Rx for Happiness

Rx for HAPPINESS

by
Pauline E. Spray

Beacon Hill Press of Kansas City
Kansas City, Missouri

Copyright, 1978
Beacon Hill Press of Kansas City

ISBN: 0-8341-0545-4

Printed in the
United States of America

To four of life's dividends:

Shari Sue,
Tami Michele,
Darla Diane, and
Beth Anne

Contents

Preface and Acknowledgments

Robert Louis Stevenson said, "There is no duty we underrate so much as the duty of being happy."

Our family is made up of individuals. As is our town. Our state. Our nation. Our world. The segments of our society reflect the moods and attitudes of the individuals within them. Wars, riots, and rebellions distinctly tell us that our planet is vitally in need of happier people.

It is indeed disturbing that many Christians are not exhibiting the happiness they should for, as never before, they need to be joyful. It is the Christians' task to show a happiness-seeking world that Jesus Christ is the Answer to the void in their lives. More and more we need to bear witness to the fact that "happy is he that hath the God of Jacob for his help, whose hope is in the Lord his God" (Ps. 146:5).

The following pages contain what I have chosen to call "a prescription for happiness." It is my prayer that these suggestions shall enable those who read to learn how to live with themselves—and others—more happily.

I am indebted to the Abingdon-Cokebury Press for granting permission to quote from Andrew Blackwood's book, *Preaching from the Bible.*

Portions of this book appeared originally in the *Herald of Holiness* published by the Nazarene Publishing House.

Again, to a host of friends and loved ones (many disguised by pseudonymns) who have afforded me illustrative material, I say, "Thank you." And beg leniency.

I have sought to give ample credit and recognition. Indulgence is sought for any cases of oversight.

My gratitude is also extended to my friend, "Aunt Marie" Mitchell, who helped out with the typing.

The words of 1 Chron. 29:13 express my feelings to my loving Heavenly Father, who grants strength, ideas, and resources for each new undertaking: "Now . . . our God, we thank thee, and praise thy glorious name."

—Pauline E. Spray

Happiness Is. . .

Shari and Tami look forward eagerly to coming to "Grandma's house," but they love their grandfather in a special way. (Given more time, Darla and Beth will also.)

Grandpa tells the girls long and fascinating tales. He buys them chewing gum and takes them to the restaurant for "coffee breaks." There they sit and chat to their hearts' content over Cokes while he sips his favorite brew and listens attentively.

Separated by many miles, we keep in touch between visits via the mail service and telephone. One winter day our daughter told us the girls had been working on their valentines, carefully choosing what to send whom and laboriously signing their names to the greetings. Tami, then five, had asked, "Mama, how do you write, 'Happiness is Grandpa'?"

While to Tami happiness is Grandpa, to another it may be a slice of bread spread lavishly with peanut butter;

—a line of freshly laundered clothes flapping merrily in the breeze;

—making the final payment on a house mortgage;

—or, communing with God in the great out-of-doors.

Just what is happiness? How do we define it?

Webster describes happiness as "a state of well-being and pleasurable satisfaction."

Happiness, it has been concluded, is what you're feeling when you want to keep on feeling that way.

Another has observed that most of us have no trouble telling when we are unhappy. However, many of us have difficulty knowing when we are happy.

One thing is certain: Happiness cannot be purchased with money. If it could, one dying millionaire would not have supposed himself to be the most miserable man on earth.

Neither does a life of ease, military glory, political power, prestige, or fame guarantee happiness. Nor does happiness come in the form of pills. Millions of dollars are spent annually on aspirins, tranquilizers, sleeping potions, and various medications, but people still wallow in gloom and despair.

Happiness is not a commodity you run out and buy with two-dollar bills or in exchange for S & H green stamps. You never find it stocked on the shelves of A & P or Montgomery Ward. It doesn't come by the bag, quart, yard, or dozen.

Happiness is a by-product. It is something you get as

a dividend when you do the right things and meet the right conditions. Sort of like getting to eat bluegills after you have had the pleasure of catching them. Or licking the icing dish after you've done your chores and been a good boy or girl.

Thousands of years ago, a man, renowned for his wisdom, recognized the way and means to true happiness. He explained, "Whoso trusteth in the Lord, happy is he" (Prov. 16:20).

David, his father, witnessed this joy when he sang, "My cup runneth over" (Ps. 23:5).

When a person has been forgiven of his sins and filled with God's Spirit, he has what it takes to live happily. Yet it is obvious and confusing that many Christians today are exhibiting far less joyfulness than they should. Wherein lies their difficulty?

The Scottish divine, Alexander Maclaren, said: "The out-and-out Christian is a joyful Christian. The half-and-half Christian is the kind of Christian that a great many of you are—little acquainted with the Lord. Why should we live halfway up the hill and swathed in the mists, when we might have an unclouded sky and a radiant sun over our heads if we would climb higher and walk in the light of His face?"

Are too many Christians living beneath their privilege? Are they relinquishing their God-given right to abundant joy because they are failing to stay close enough to Jesus? To trust and heed His Word as they should? Are they failing to follow His rules for spiritual and mental health? Are they neglecting to "take" His prescription for happiness?

The Lord has provided for everything the Christian needs to enjoy life. He offers freedom from guilt, fear, worry, resentment, and despair. He teaches us how to live unselfishly, what to think about, how to bring meaning and purpose to life. For every problem, He offers a solution.

Certainly life is not all fluff and down, not even for the

child of God. However, the Lord bids us exchange our spirit of heaviness for His repose. Nights of weeping may come, but they should be followed by mornings of joyfulness.

I, too, once wrestled with the matter of happiness. My struggle took place years ago during a period of exhaustion and depression. For many days I was plagued with questions: What is happiness? How can I know if I am happy or not? How do I go about being happy? Does God want me to be joyful?

An entry in my diary reveals both my devotion and my perplexity: "As oft before, the tormentor told me, 'Your husband doesn't need you, and the girls could get along as well without you.' But . . . I must live for Jesus . . . so others can see Him in me."

To add to my distress, a highly-esteemed leader in the church, regarded as deeply spiritual by many, continually harped on the virtues of bearing burdens.

Young, inexperienced, extremely conscientious, and fatigued, I was driven more urgently to intensify my quest. Does God want His children to carry burdens? Or, does He want us to be carefree? What is His will?

In one of my husband's books I found help. According to Andrew Blackwood in *Preaching from the Bible*, "Being happy is the minister's chief business here below. . . . Living as he does amid many people who are not happy, he should show them what it means to be a Christian."[1]

How could my minister-husband be happy if I were not? If it is his "chief business," I decided, it must be mine also. And in God's Word I found what I needed. The ingredients in His prescription are the best. His medication never fails if taken as directed.

Happiness is not only the Christian's privilege, it is his duty.

Washington Irving said: "Surely happiness is reflective, like the light from heaven: and every countenance, bright with smiles and glowing with innocent enjoyment, is a mirror, transmitting to others the rays of a supreme and ever-shining benevolence."

As never before, Christians (both clergy and laity) need to be filled with the joy Christ gives so they can show the needy, seeking world in which we live what happiness really is.

Happiness Is . . .

God's Word

Woodrow Wilson said, "When you have read the Bible, you will know it is the Word of God, because you will have found it the key to your own heart, your own happiness and your own duty."

Another president of the United States, Theodore Roosevelt, said, "If a man is not familiar with the Bible, he has suffered a loss which he had better make all possible haste to correct."

The Bible is the Christian's guide to spiritual prosperity and emotional tranquility. It contains all the rules needed for the enjoyment of mental health. Within its pages are found God's prescription for happiness. Not only does God bid us to "be . . . holy as I am holy," He also expects us to live with enjoyment as well as purity.

The Psalmist said, "Be glad in the Lord, and rejoice, ye righteous: and shout for joy, all ye that are upright in heart" (Ps. 32:11).

Many Christians lack joy because they do not immerse themselves in God's Word and believe it implicitly. These Christians need to specifically ask the Lord for a faith that will enable them to accept His Word with a childlike trust.

George Muller said his unprecedented life of faith began when he made the Bible his sole standard of judgment in spiritual things. It caused his soul to grow as no other book had.

Perusing and assimilating God's Word is vitally essential to a productive Christian life. "Faith cometh by hearing . . . the word of God" (Rom. 10:17); and, "all scripture is . . . profitable for doctrine, for reproof, for correction, for instruction in righteousness" (2 Tim. 3:16-17).

The Bible sets forth the Heavenly Father's impartial plan of salvation—deliverance from eternal damnation and the assurance of everlasting life—for all. It points the way to freedom from guilt, fear, and hostility. It offers hope for depression and despair. It tells us what to think about, how to control and direct our activities, and how to find meaning, purpose, and fulfillment in life.

In His Word, God gives recognition to our individual worth. He reveals His love, care, and concern for each of us. He assures us of His personalized comfort, sympathy, and understanding. And He has pledged to never leave nor forsake us.

God's Word inspires confidence and its promises give security—two things needed by all Christians, especially those who are bothered by insecurity and overconscientiousness. It contains the instruction so vitally needed by people who are lacking in judgment and initiative.

It is true that seared consciences come by wholesale lots today. There is a great slackening of moral convictions everywhere, even among many so-called Christians. "Anything goes" seems to be the accepted rule among many. Still there are some Christians who are hindered spiritually and emotionally by unusually sensitive and overworked consciences.

Certainly it is far better to be born with a temperament that lends itself to overly conscientiousness than it is to possess an insensitivity to spiritual matters. I know from experience how much agony an overly strict conscience can cause, however.

Overly conscientious people suffer acutely from fear, doubts, misgivings, guilts, fanatical suggestions, and the pressures thrust on them by others. Many go through life being led by stronger-minded, more persuasive and self-confident personalities. Individuals well advanced in years may still feel guilty when they do something they suspect would be frowned on by an authority in their past.

People who live according to the persuasions of others are often unhappy. They may be difficult to get along with because they (consciously or subconsciously) resent being told what to do. They secretly long to follow their own choices. Their resentment may be expressed through fault-finding, criticalness, gossiping, envy, or jealousy.

Because overly conscientious people lack the stamina and self-confidence to think for themselves, they especially need to learn firsthand what God has to say to them in His Word. And they need to learn to trust Him for personalized direction, seeking His will concerning what is right and what is wrong for them as individuals. Paul said, "Let every man be fully persuaded in his own mind" (Rom. 14:5).

Being overly conscientious does not necessarily make one genuinely spiritual. It is not simply what we do or don't do that brings divine approval. True spirituality involves the hidden motives of the heart. God wants our whole-hearted devotion, a total submissiveness to His will, and implicit trust and obedience. "The kingdom of God is not meat and drink; but righteousness, and peace, and joy in the Holy Ghost. For he that in these things serveth Christ is acceptable to God" (Rom. 14:17).

When an individual reaches adulthood, he need not feel guilty if his ideas concerning nonessentials differ from those of someone he reveres, or has revered in the past.

I can remember hearing my grandmother ask Mom plaintively, "Mary, can't you at least wear your sleeves below your elbows?" Mom's usual just-above-the-elbow length distressed Grandma, who rolled her wrist-length sleeves up to an inch below her elbows—far enough to wash the dishes or knead the bread. However, as soon as danger of soiling them was over, down her sleeves came, the wrinkles smoothed out by her workworn hands.

Although we need not feel in bondage to them or their ideas, this does not mean we should resent or dishonor those who served as "voices of authority" to us in the past. Neither should we discard everything we learned from previous teachings. Nor should we take an independent, rebellious attitude toward those we may feel have misguided us or made life hard on us.

Let us remember that "love never faileth," and keep a humble and forgiving attitude. We should be grateful for the acceptable training we received. And we should accept the advice of the sagacious in the present.

Far too many are living independently of the rules of God, home, church, and the law, and are experiencing frustration. Liberty and happiness are found within restrictions.

"We ought to obey God rather than men," the early Christians declared. And they were right, for in the final analysis, it is God to whom we shall give a final account. He must become the ultimate voice of authority to each soul. From His Word must come our answers and guidance.

Ofttimes people who are raised in the church and have accepted their parents' religion as a matter of fact are faced later in life with a unique problem. They may find themselves asking, "Do I believe this simply because I was taught it? Or do I believe this because God has revealed it as His will in His Word? Is it His will for me personally?

All my life I was submissive and docile, accepting without mental reservation what I was taught, never learning to dig into the meaning of things or to think for myself. Finally I realized that I, and only I, shall give account to God. Regardless of the rightness of my upbringing (and I wholeheartedly thank God for righteous and loving parents), I wanted to learn for myself what God expected of me as a person, an individual.

So in desperation I turned to God's Word with total trust and abandon. I found what I was looking for. It brought healing for body, soul, and mind. As the Psalmist said, "It is good for me that I have been afflicted; that I might learn thy statues" (Ps. 119:71), for "unless thy law had been my delights, I should then have perished in mine affliction" (Ps. 119:92).

"Happiness is . . . God's Word."

Happiness Is . . .

Keeping Close to God

Hannah Whitall Smith, author of the devotional classic *The Christian's Secret of a Happy Life*, has been called "a happy passenger in the chariot of God."[2]

And this description should apply to all Christians.

The Psalmist said, "Let all those that seek thee rejoice and be glad in thee" (Ps. 70:4).

Nehemiah reminds us that "the joy of the Lord is [our] strength" (Neh. 8:10).

Larry drives a truck the year around, delivering oil to farmers throughout a wide area of southwestern Michigan. His ever-present smile bears testimony to his fellowship with the Divine. "He rides right there with me," he said, "right there in the seat."

Another young person, a college student, had missed several midweek services because of night courses. "I missed church, but I was never away from Him," she said with a note of definite victory.

Keeping close to God is the only way to insure true and enduring happiness.

Bishop Massillon said, "God should be the object of

all our desires, the end of all our actions, the principle of all our affections, and the governing power of our whole souls."

We keep close to God by spending time alone with Him. A wise way to begin the day is by conversing with the Lord. The longer private devotions are postponed, the easier they are omitted altogether. We cannot expect life to run smoothly unless we include Jesus Christ in all our plans and activities. (Someone has suggested that we set the tone for the day by the attitude we assume during the first five minutes upon awakening. Surely beginning the day in communion with Jesus is the best pacesetter of all.)

Prayer renews, revitalizes, unctionizes, and connects us with God's wonderful Spirit, His love and His goodness. It is the lifeline of the Christian. Without it, he withers and dies. Rubbing elbows with skeptical unbelievers day after day and expending the nervous energy needed to combat the forces of Satan is exacting and exhausting. Christians need spiritual renewal as surely as they need physical nourishment and rest.

Jesus withdrew to the wilderness to pray after ministering to the multitude. If He, the divine Son of God, felt the need for spiritual, mental, and physical renewal, how much more should we?

Sometimes it takes Christians a long time to get in touch with the Lord when they go to prayer. The reason is they get too far out of touch with Him in between their prayer times. The secret of being able to contact God's presence readily is to keep a sense of His nearness with us at all times.

If we neglect practicing good manners, we soon find ourselves at a loss when wanting to impress someone special. If we persist in putting our elbows on the table at home, the first thing we know we're doing it in the restaurant or banquet hall. To maintain good table manners one must habitually use them.

So it is with practicing the presence of God. By deliberately keeping close to Him, it finally becomes a way of life.

While hanging up the clothes one day, I thought: Isn't it wonderful to be able to fellowship with the Lord as I go about my work instead of having to wait to talk to Him when I am on my knees in a closet somewhere!

I used to pray in the morning and then with a "Lord-it's -been-nice-talking-to-You-but-so-long-until-tonight" attitude, I left the room. How grateful I am to have learned better. Now His presence goes with me to the basement to wash and hang up the clothes, to empty the garbage, to the sink while doing the dishes, to the grocery store, to water my flowers, everywhere. And it makes all the difference in the world.

"How can I think about God all the time?" you ask. "I have many other things on my mind, too, you know! How can a person dwell on more than one thing at a time and do it successfully?"

Certainly we must concentrate on our daily tasks. Many a factory worker has been injured because of a lack of attention. Many a kettle of beans has burned for the same reason.

However, we can maintain an awareness of God's presence with us at all times by deliberately bringing Him back into our thoughts from time to time. By consciously making a practice of doing this, it becomes a habit.

The Lord is pleased when we do this. He wants to be an integral part of our conversations, our business dealings, schoolteaching, banking transactions, gas-pumping, baby-changing, children-spanking, writing, professional services, or whatever.

According to an article in *Guideposts*, the world-famous teacher, author, and linguist Dr. Frank Laubach, said his work lacked color and was unproductive until he started "practicing the presence of God." It changed his life.[3]

A lady from Wichita, Kans., wrote me that she decided to talk to God after undergoing several surgeries and cobalt treatments for a tumor on her pituitary gland. "While in the hospital," she said, "I never put an Amen on my prayers because I wanted Him available at all times."

For over 40 years the soul of Brother Lawrence, the 17th-century monk, was filled with so many joys that at times he was forced to "moderate them," he said. This barefooted saint, working among the pots and pans in the monastery kitchen, "practiced the presence of God" by recognizing that God was intimately with him at all times. He continually conversed with the Lord and willfully brought Him back into his mind whenever it strayed. It is said that Brother Lawrence hardly ever turned from the Presence of God despite his humble and busy life.

Someone wrote: "There must have been something rare in a monastery cook that a Grand Vicar would listen to his talk and should beg of him not the recipe for a sauce but his secret of a happy life."[4]

Many things in life are fleeting, but Jesus promised, "Lo, I am with you alway, even unto the end of the world" (Matt. 28:20). His Word cannot fail. Joy comes with that recognition.

"Happiness is . . . keeping close to God."

Happiness Is . . .

Living the Yielded Life

A minister was visiting in a home where there were two little girls. The older was reserved and very dignified. The younger, vivacious and uninhibited.

While the meal was being prepared, the men visited in the living room. Eventually the mother gave permission for the youngsters to call their father and his guest to the table.

"Daddy, dinner's ready!" the younger child cried, bounding into her father's arms and hugging him. Then, looking at her sister who watched in silence, she teased, "I've got all there is of Daddy."

At that, the father reached out and drew the timid lass into his arms also. "You may have all there is of Daddy," she retorted, "but Daddy has all there is of me."

Our Heavenly Father wants all there is of us, likewise. He will settle for no less than a complete consecration, a total yielding of our will to His will.

The Virgin Mary expressed perfect submission to the will of God when she exclaimed, "Behold the handmaid of the Lord; be it according to thy word" (Luke 1:38).

Solomon said, "The king's heart is in the hand of the

Lord, as the rivers of water: he turneth it whithersoever he will" (Prov. 21:1).

Dr. James Madge said, "Happy are they that become nothing (in their own estimation). In other words, happy are they that give themselves away to Christ, and then always abide in Him."

This is what Paul meant when he wrote to the Romans: "I beseech you . . . brethren . . . present your bodies a living sacrifice, holy, acceptable unto God, which is your reasonable service. And be not conformed to this world: but be ye transformed by the renewing of your mind, that ye may prove what is that good, and acceptable, and perfect, will of God" (Rom. 12:1-2).

Consecration is not a once-in-a-lifetime but a continuing experience. The way to receive the fullness of the Holy Spirit is through total and complete surrender to the whole will of God. And the way to keep filled with His Spirit is to keep a continual yieldedness to the whole will of God.

We might say that when we yield ourselves "unto God, as those alive from the dead, and [our] members as instruments of righteousness unto God," we "consecrate on credit." This means we surrender everything to God that we know at the moment, plus everything He may reveal to us in the future.

L. Guy Nees said, "Surrender means the surrender of as much of myself as I know right now, to as much of Christ as I know at this moment."

During my teens, I surrendered my life to God as best I knew how. But I have had to bring my consecration up-to-date more than once since then. Shortly after our marriage, while visiting my grandparents, I went to the room directly over the one where I was physically born. Kneeling beside Grandma's straw tick bed, I surrendered my whole self anew to Him and received the witness that He accepted my offering and filled me with His Spirit.

Nor did my surrendering end there. Later on in my life, the Lord asked me to give up a certain thing I earnestly wanted to do. After a genuine struggle, I completely and unreservedly yielded to the will of God—and peace came. Since then, keeping surrendered unconditionally has been easier. I have found that daily yielding to the Lord prevents Satan from injecting self-will or driving wedges into my consecration.

God doesn't promise us that His will is always the easiest way. Nor does He promise us that in carrying out His plan for our lives, we shall not be called upon to suffer or to make sacrifices. But He does promise grace for every need and strength for our weaknesses.

"Know assuredly that you must live a dying life; and the more anyone dies to himself, so much the more does he begin to live unto God" (Author unknown).

The initial surrendering of our will to God makes all subsequent yielding an easier task.

We have always been a close-knit family. Now both of our daughters are married and we are separated by many miles. Christmas is a glorious time of reunion.

"Mama, don't feel too badly when we all leave this year," Sybil pleaded.

"No, I won't," I promised. "Each of us is where the Lord wants us to be. You, Wayne, and the little girls are in the Lord's will in Kansas City. Sue and David are in the Lord's will at Deckerville (since this incident, Darla and Beth have joined them). And Daddy and I are where the Lord wants us. So this is the way it must be. And we shall be content with things as they are." This assurance made it much easier for all of us to say good-by when departure time came.

We often visited Mrs. Broadbent as she lay dying with cancer. Over and over she said, "God's will must be done."

And she never retracted her declaration of total submission to the will of God.

Jesus taught us to pray, "Our Father which art in heaven, Hallowed be thy name. Thy kingdom come. Thy will be done in earth, as it is in heaven" (Matt. 6:9-10).

God, the Father, is the supreme authority in heaven. The angels bow in submission to Him. They are in total subjection. His word is law. His every wish is carried out. No one puts up an argument. Satan once tried but was cast out of heaven for his attempt.

God's will must be done on earth—as it is done in heaven. Resistance brings trouble and tension. "Holding out" on God invites conflict and stress. Some of the most miserable people on earth are trying to hold on to God with one hand and to their selfish will with the other. But it is only as we love Him with our "all" that we are freed of inner conflict. It is then we find peace of mind, rest of soul, and personality integration.

"If you want success and happiness, you must give self, all of self," I heard a dedicated Christian say. This man gave up a lucrative position in engineering with the Oldsmobile division of General Motors to become a maintainance man in Africa.

I was in one of the final services he attended before leaving with his family for missionary work overseas. In a gesture symbolizing his consecration, he stepped forward and laid a wrench on the altar.

"Here it is, Lord," he said. "It's me. Take all."

Man was created with the instinctive need to belong wholly and completely to God. Only His indwelling Presence can satisfy this need and bring fulfillment.

"Happiness is . . . living the yielded life."

Happiness Is . . .

Living with a Purpose

When our happy-go-lucky, little granddaughter was asked, "What are you going to be when you grow up?" she spontaneously replied, "A nothing."

Coming from a five-year-old, that was cute. However, our "Great Society," as President Lyndon Johnson called it, is presently challenged by too many "nobodies" who are declining to accept responsibility. The very thing they are seeking is eluding them. True happiness comes only with purposeful living. Without a driving, real-life interest, one wanders aimlessly like an autumn leaf driven by the wind.

Interestingly enough, an English philosopher of the 18th century, Thomas Carlyle, said, "The man without a purpose is like a ship without a rudder—a waif, a nothing, a no-man. Have a purpose in life, and, having it, throw some strength of mind and muscle into your work as God has given you."

In *How to Make a Habit of Succeeding*, Mack R. Douglas insists that a dynamic purpose is the key to personal success. Happiness is not dependent on external circumstances and surroundings, but by constantly progressing toward a worthy life purpose.

When he was 10 years old, Henry F. Ashurst signed his name in one of his schoolbooks. Under it he wrote, "United States Senator from Arizona." While working as a lumberjack, hod-carrier, clerk, cowboy, and lawyer, he never lost sight of his life's purpose. Eventually, perseverance paid off and his dream became a reality.

Dr. David Starr Jordon, onetime president of Stanford University, said, "The world steps aside to let any man pass who knows where he is going."

Recently some friends of ours left the pastorate to enter full-time evangelism. In doing so, they moved into their own home—the result of much planning, diligent management, and unyielding perseverance.

It all began many years ago while Harold was working in his garden. The Lord impressed him with an idea and seemed to indicate to him that he should begin building a house for use at some future date.

For most people, constructing an abode would be quite a normal procedure. With our friends it wasn't so simple. Serving in the pastoral ministry meant managing on a limited income and making frequent locational changes. But having received the "green light," Harold proceeded to draw up plans and build his house in sections as the Lord supplied the ways and means.

Almost immediately, people began giving him lumber. Other supplies were purchased at bargain prices. Friends offered their physical assistance. Relatives donated a plot of land on which to build and gave Harold permission to store the unassembled sections, which were transported in installments over many miles, in their large, vacant barn. (By the way, when finally assembled, these portions fit almost perfectly.)

Seventeen years later, Harold and Orpha moved into

their lovely home, the result of striving to reach their goals through faith and diligent effort.

Long ago I searched my soul to determine my life purpose. The following words defined it then and now: "My soul's sincere desire is to be a clear channel through which the Holy Spirit can move with absolute freedom to help, bless, and inspire others to the greatest extent possible."

Since my cardinal purpose included many phases of life—personal devotement, husband, children, church, my writing—I also set secondary goals for these areas because they were involved in, as Paul said, "reaching forth unto those things which are before."

The apostle Paul himself expressed purpose when he went on to say, "I press toward the mark for the prize of the high calling of God in Christ Jesus" (Phil. 3:13-14).

Jesus said, "Seek ye first the kingdom of God, and his righteouness; and all these things shall be added unto you" (Matt. 6:33).

What are you living for? What is your ultimate purpose for existence? Have you set goals which will enable you to attain that purpose?

Why not seek until you find God's design and will for your life? Define your intention. Your dream. Set goals that will help you to achieve "the mark" you have set. Visualize yourself, not as you believe yourself to be now, but as you wish to become. Then, keeping your eyes on the prize, persevere until your desire becomes a reality.

Disraeli said, "The secret of success is constancy of purpose."

And according to the great-grandson of the fiery preacher Jonathan Edwards, Tryon Edwards: "Seek happiness for its own sake, and you will not find it; seek for duty, and happiness will follow as the shadow comes with the sunshine."

"Happiness is . . . living with a purpose."

Happiness Is . . .

Self-understanding

Joy, someone has suggested, is Jesus, first; Others, second, and, Yourself, last.

Jesus told us the way to "inherit eternal life" is to "love the Lord thy God with all thy heart, and with all thy soul, and with all thy strength, and with all thy mind; and thy neighbour as thyself" (Luke 10:27).

We have discussed giving God first place in our lives. We are now ready to look at the remaining two requisites for joyful living. Before we pursue the matter of loving others, let us first consider the aspects of loving "thyself."

"Know thyself," Socrates advised. It is by understanding himself that man is able to understand and live more successfully with his fellowmen.

"In order to judge of the inside of others, study your own; for men in general are very much alike, and though one has one prevailing passion, and another has another, yet their operations are much the same; and whatever engages or disgusts, pleases, or offends you in others, will engage, disgust, please or offend others in you," said Philip Chesterfield, 18th-century orator and wit.

King Solomon recognized the role self-understanding plays in the matter of happiness. He observed, "Understanding is a wellspring of life unto him that hath it" (Prov. 16:22).

Human beings are more or less alike because all possess the same basic urges and needs. Still each is also unique, a distinct, one-of-a-kind creation, fashioned by the imaginative hand of God. By understanding our individual differences, we are better able to make the most of what God has given us.

Understanding one's aptitudes, capabilities, and strengths enables one to make a greater contribution to life. Understanding one's weaknesses and limitations prevents discouragement, frustration, and failure.

Self-understanding precedes healing. Before a person can receive spiritual satisfaction, he must recognize that he is a sinner and in need of God's forgiveness. Self-understanding is also necessary for the relief of tension, the greatest cause of illness today.

In a newspaper column, Dr. Joseph G. Molner observed that "nerves" affect, to some extent, the great majority of people. For some, it becomes a distressing problem. The real cure for most cases of emotional distress comes with finding out the truth about oneself, accepting what one finds, and then changing one's habits and attitudes through discipline.

Self-understanding doesn't come easily, however. It is difficult to be absolutely honest and frank when it comes to analyzing ourselves. We tend to see ourselves, not as we actually are, but as we wish to be or as we hope others see us. While having his portrait done, Cromwell said, "Paint me just as I am—wart and all." To truly know ourselves, we must face up to both the good and the bad, in other words, "warts and all."

How wonderful for the Christian to have the assistance

of the Holy Spirit in this! Prayer brings divine revelations. The Bible also furnishes a ready source of illumination.

"Through thy precepts I get understanding," noted the Psalmist (Ps. 119:104).

Additional instruction and help is available through the works and experiences of others. A young mother suffering from fatigue and worry wrote us: "I've been reading *The Art of Understanding Yourself*[6] . . . It has really helped. . . . I'm beginning to see that I'm not as bad off as I thought I was."

Talking with other people often brings enlightenment. This same person said: "One afternoon while riding home from school with a teacher friend, we started talking about nervous problems. She told about some of her own experiences, and also about some friends of hers, and I was totally surprised. Her experiences and those of others were exactly like my own. It was a revelation."

Writing an autobiography sometimes proves helpful. Recalling past experiences often brings understanding. When I was young, my mother gave me a birthday party, a very nice one with many little friends present to help celebrate the occasion. That is, everything was lovely until we played a game in which the one who was "it" was called a dummy. My turn came. Everyone laughed. They clapped their hands, danced up and down, and shouted gleefully, "Pauline is a dummy! Pauline is a dummy!" Their laughter and focalized attention proved too much for my sensitive nature. I burst into tears and refused to be comforted.

Inside the house my bewildered mother took me in her arms and assured me my friends were laughing *with*, not *at*, me. However, the stigma of that hysterical incident left an indelible imprint on my mind. In later years while going through periods of stress, this troublesome sensation returned. After understanding why I was bothered in this way, I was able to ask the Lord for special assistance in overcoming it.

The recalling of earlier experiences may help us understand others, likewise. A young schoolteacher wondered why children so often dislike the subject of reading. Reflecting on her own childhood, she discovered an answer.

Dale's older brother had been ill most of the winter he was in the first grade. Their mother tried tutoring him at home, but he was slow and his mother, impatient. "What is that word?" she demanded irritably. "What did I say it was?" After repeated reprimands, the lad burst into tears.

Dale loved her brother very much and she decided that anything that hurt him must be distasteful, so she began school with a chip on her shoulder. She hated reading, too.

"If we could read the secret history of our enemies, we should find in each man's life sorrow and suffering enough to disarm all hostility," said Henry Wadsworth Longfellow.

Self-understanding enables us to appreciate and sympathize with others. It makes loving the unlovable easier.

As Solomon said, understanding is a "wellspring of life," but even so, introspection can be carried too far. Therefore this word of caution is injected here. Overindulgence in self-examination can increase self-centeredness, sap one's energy, and stop one's progress. Judicious control, as in all of life, is needed. After taking an honest, frank, thorough inventory of himself, a person must move ahead, profiting by what he has found, and living by faith and with love.

Without reasonable introspection and understanding, however, one cannot enjoy self-mastery. "Self-mastery requires a full knowledge of one's self, or at least a steadily growing knowledge. . . . Increasing knowledge leads the way to increasing mastery, and should lead to a greater reverence," said S. D. Gordon in *Quiet Talks on Personal Problems.*[7]

And the early German saint, Thomas à Kempis, said, "An humble knowledge of thyself is a surer way to God than a deep search after learning."

"Happiness is . . . self-understanding."

Happiness Is . . .

Self-acceptance

We enjoy our travels much more when we harmonize with the bumps and jolts, blending into the rhythm of the ride. If we stiffen out every time the driver applies the brakes, if we resist every lurch and swerve the car makes, we are worn to a frazzle by the time we reach our destination.

Likewise, our journey through life is less strenuous and more enjoyable if we take a yielding attitude toward the inevitable. Resistance causes tension. We need to change what can be changed, but we need to learn to accept those things we can do nothing about.

If we are to enjoy happiness, we must accept our personal uniqueness. Personality is the sum total of many things—physical traits, temperament, degree of intelligence, strengths, weaknesses, habits, experiences, ambitions, hopes, and dreams. Individuality is that certain something that distinguishes one person from another. It is our personalized "identification tag."

In the beginning the Lord created man in His image. Since God is unique, for "there is one God; and there is none other but he" (Mark 12:32), it naturally follows that man, too, is unique. Each human being is a one-of-a-kind creation. And each has his own special niche to fill.

Individuality makes for variety on earth. If each person possessed only the "standardized equipment"—the five senses, instincts, skeleton, glands, blood, muscles, nervous system—if each looked and acted exactly alike, this planet would be a monotonous place on which to live.

God's love of variety is revealed in nature—the snowflakes and leaves, for example, no two of which are alike. It is further demonstrated in the diverse and appurtenant characteristics of the human races. Whether the labels are accurate or not, we have all heard about the stoicism of the Japanese, the easygoing manner of the Negro, the cunning of the American Indian, the pugnaciousness of the Irish, the emotionalism of the Italian, the shrewdness of the Jewish, and the frugality of the Scotsman.

People view the matter of individuality differently, however. Some pride themselves on being "a distinct entity," as the dictionary calls us. But being unlike their peers gives rise to adverse feelings of anxiety and distress in others.

Teenagers, especially, find it difficult to be individualistic. They seek (at great expense to their appearance and pocketbooks) to look and act like their peers. Usually this tendency decreases somewhat with age and experience. But not always. Many adults are knocking themselves out trying to keep up with the neighbors next door or down the block. Others try frustratingly to measure up to unrealistic mental images and ideals they have acquired.

I greatly admire tall, willowy, chic women. Nevertheless, I know I shall always be the "pleasingly plump and pleasant," motherly type of person. Nature decreed it. I may as well accept it gracefully.

Secondly, we need to accept our temperamental differences. Some people are tranquilly phlegmatic. Nothing seems to irritate them. Nor move them. Others are restless and energetic. They cannot sit by the hour drinking coffee and "chewing the fat." Choleric individuals have to keep occupied.

People who are bothered by nervousness especially need to understand that we are not expected to behave alike. When we try to duplicate another's style of living, we run into trouble. If monotony wears on our nerves, we should avoid as much of it as possible. If one finds that his line of work is unsuited to his well-being, it is time to change his occupation.

Then, too, we must learn to accept our limitations. This was clearly illustrated to me one day while I sat looking out on beautiful Grand Traverse Bay in northern Michigan. The blue-gray waters extended into the hazy horizon. Dozens of majestic swans rested on the glassy surface while a lone female mallard swam among them.

"How does that duck feel?" I wondered. "Is she aware of her plainness among those beautiful creatures?"

A duck can never be a swan. But a swan can never be a duck. A swan is more striking in appearance, but it cannot travel as far. Both have their limitations. And so do we. They accept theirs. We must accept ours, too.

We also need to accept our imperfections. Because of Adam's fall, we all suffer. Some more. Some less. There is no such thing as a perfectly adjusted individual anywhere. While our motives may be the purest, we must recognize that we can never be entirely free from mental and physical flaws.

In *Problems of the Spirit-filled Life*, William S. Deal explains that some people are shocked to learn that there is no such thing as a perfectly "normal" human being, psychologically speaking. Everyone is subject to fluctuating emotions. Sometimes we are above normal. At other times, we fall below normal. Being "normal" is somewhere between two extremes.

Maladjustments (complexes) grow out of the habits and attitudes we develop, usually in early life, while endeavoring to adjust to our environment and circumstances.

The task of the Christian is to seek to overcome his weaknesses with the help of the Lord. And he should capitalize on his strengths. Then he can be different—as different as the Lord desires him to be. He can be himself and stop seeking to imitate others. This brings freedom.

Over a century ago Sidney Smith—an English clergyman, author, and wit—made a judicious observation. He said: "It was not very long before I made two very useful discoveries: First; that all mankind were not solely employed in observing me—a belief that all young people have; and next, that shamming was of no use—that the world was very clear sighted and soon estimated a man at his true value. This cured me, and I determined to be natural and let the world find it out."

A sign of good mental health, we're told, is the ability to take a tolerant, easygoing attitude not only toward oneself but toward others also.

Some people continually look for weaknesses in others in an effort to console themselves about their own. Often the individuals who irk us most are those who possess the same traits we dislike in ourselves.

Self-acceptance does not mean resignation or satisfaction. It means we have found the weak areas in our lives that need correcting or strengthening. And the Christian who strives to be more like the Lord daily will keep "darning" and "mending" until he exchanges his earthly garment for a white robe in God's eternal habitation.

"Thy will be done." This was Jesus' prayer. And if we are to enjoy happiness, it must be ours, also.

If he is to glorify the Lord, a Christian's surrender must

include the willingness to be different. This is because God made us as we are, to be used by Him as we are, for a specific purpose. If we fail to utilize our individuality, we fail to fill the distinctive place in His plan that He intended we should. In doing so, we shrivel up. We lose a blessing. And we disappoint our Maker.

"As every man hath received the gift, even so minister the same one to another, as good stewards of the manifold grace of God" (1 Pet. 4:10).

"Happiness is . . . self-acceptance."

Happiness Is . . .

Self-esteem

Don't go around calling yourself a poor worm of the dust, or someone will put you on his fishhook," I heard someone say.

Many people ruin their chances for a happy life by continually "putting down" themselves. A proper sense of self-esteem is essential for enjoyable and productive living.

In *Psycho-Cybernetics*, Dr. Maxwell Maltz says persons lacking in self-esteem are thin-skinned, easily hurt, self-centered, self-concerned, and hard to live with. Because they are overly sensitive and self-conscious, they apply the criticisms (or supposed barbs) of others to themselves—even if they are not intended for them. These people are also subject to envy, jealousy, and criticalness. They tear down others in an effort to build up themselves.

A lack of self-esteem makes one feel one never quite measures up, never does quite enough, is not as qualified or worthy as the next fellow.

Physical defects cause many to suffer a lack of confidence. Nevertheless, some of the most interesting and charming persons are those who have triumphed over imperfections. One of the best read individuals I know has such poor eyesight that she was educated in a school for the blind. One of the happiest and best adjusted children I have known was one of the homeliest.

A lack of education may cause one to feel inferior to those holding academic degrees. (This personal lack has caused me not a little discomfort in times past, but, since both of our daughters have become college graduates, I derive great comfort and pleasure from the fact that they still ask "Mama's" advice at times.)

Let us remember that the libraries offer a free education to all who will avail themselves of their services. Furthermore, we learn through living, and experience is still the best teacher of all.

Authorities believe feelings of inferiority begin early in life, although they may be aggravated by repeated failure in later years. Sometimes parents pass on their own inferiorities to their offspring. Also, parents often fail to express affection, causing their children to feel insecure, unloved, and unwanted. Then, too, feelings of inadequacy may come from the suggestions and impatience of both parents and teachers.

The first step in overcoming many of our difficulties is in understanding why we feel or react as we do. When we have acquired an adequate insight into a problem, we are well on our way toward resolving it.

Dr. William Sadler believes people who are lacking in self-esteem should get involved in religion, literature, science, philosophy, and art. He suggests, in *Theory and Practice of Psychiatry*, that they pursue worthwhile and satisfying occupations, strive to reach goals that are reachable, engage in creative efforts, and put forth an intelligent and persistent effort to adjust to life's situations. They should become truly interested in others. And, they need to learn how to get the most out of life.

To be happy we need also to look at our pluses frankly and honestly.

During the course of an interview, the Secretary of the Navy was being questioned concerning the relative strength of the United States fleet and its adjunct arsenal. He assured the panel that the navy was well equipped and its personnel competent. Then, almost as an aside, he added, "It is all right to look at our problems, but we should also look at our successes."

This applies also to us as individuals. It is unhealthy to dwell only on our faults and failures. Negative thinking lowers self-respect and leads to defeat. Contrarily, over-estimating one's good points is also unsatisfactory. (A song leader intending to sing, "I'm so happy and here's the reason why," sang instead, "We're so happy and I'm the reason why.") Therefore we must endeavor to take a realistic view of both our weaknesses and strengths.

The person in need of more self-esteem should recognize his successes, giving thanks to God for His assistance, specifically praising Him for each degree of progress made.

Practicing good manners and social graces also increases one's confidence. Everyone profits by dressing properly and with care. Habitually thinking of others and trying to set them at ease is a virtue worth cultivating.

Furthermore, each individual needs to be able to do at least one thing well. Few of us possess outstanding talents or abilities. Yet through persistent effort we can develop what we have and make a worthy contribution to the world. The Christian should view his capabilities as gifts from God and feel a keen obligation to use them for His glory. "Let a man so account of himself as the minister of Christ and a steward" (1 Cor. 4:1).

Finally, the person with a low estimate of himself should understand that in God's sight every individual is important, wanted, and loved. No one is esteemed unworthy. No one is rejected or exempted.

In the beginning "the Lord God formed man of the

dust of the ground, and breathed into his nostrils the breath of life; and man became a living soul" (Gen. 2:7).

Man's soul is of infinite worth. Jesus implied that it is worth more than all the world when He asked, "What is a man profited, if he shall gain the whole world, and lose his own soul? or what shall a man give in exchange for his soul?" (Matt. 16:26).

Peter reminds us, "Ye were not redeemed with corruptible things, as silver and gold . . . but with the precious blood of Christ, as a lamb without blemish and without spot" (1 Pet. 1:18-19).

And the best-loved verse in the Bible assures us that "God so loved the world, that he gave his only begotten Son, that *whosoever* believeth in him should not perish, but have everlasting life" (John 3:16, italics mine).

The person who has been adopted into the family of God should understand that he is a chosen vessel, very special and precious, an heir to unlimited resources. He is somebody! Let him never forget it!

I was thinking along this line one day several years ago when I wrote the following:

I am very fond of pretty glassware. Hobnail and milk glass are among my favorites. Yes, the kind I like are more expensive, and needless to say, I seldom am able to purchase any for myself. However, I sometimes purchase a piece to give as a gift to a relative or friend. It is a personal pleasure to be able to visit one of the stores in our nice little town where they handle many beautiful pieces of glassware and china. Sometimes, even though I am unable to buy anything, I manage to get up the courage to go in and just browse around.

One day while looking over the beautiful display of dishes, I began to feel rather self-conscious. A lady, very obviously quite wealthy and somewhat snobbish in her attitude and appearance, was looking over the display, too.

But with her it seemed to be a matter of choosing what she liked best, while with me it was a matter of "just looking."

I felt as though my purse were made of glass, too, and that she knew I could not buy anything. At first it seemed to me that she was silently asking: What business have you in here? You haven't any money. You cannot buy any of this. You are a *nobody* and you know it. This is no place for people of your kind to be wasting time. What are you doing here, anyway?

But instead of slinking out of her presence like a whipped animal, I held up my head and began to feel very important, for a wonderful revelation came to me. It was something like this: Lady, you don't know who I am. I am *Somebody*. I'm a child of the Heavenly King. That makes me a princess. I have royal blood in *my* veins. Yes, *my* Father is very wealthy, too. He owns the cattle on a thousand hills. In fact, He owns the world and everything therein. Greater still, He created the universe, the visible and the invisible, to His liking.

Since I have been adopted into His family, I am an heir to heavenly treasures. Jesus has gone to prepare a mansion for me that will exceed anything human mind can imagine, and it will not be any run-of-the-mill affair, either. It will be custom-built—just for me. I may not have much silver and gold in this present world, but I'll never be able to count, or even estimate, the riches my Heavenly Father has in store for me. They are waiting for me in heaven now, and some day I expect to claim them for my own.

Soon I began to feel very sorry for the lady. Christian love filled my heart for her. She did not have happiness displayed on her countenance. The lovely things she could purchase would never bring her the abundant joy I had within my heart. I realized how fortunate I am. I *am* a child of the King. I *am* a princess. Yes, I'm Somebody!

"Happiness is . . . self-esteem."

Happiness Is . . .

Self-control

Autumn, in my opinion, is the most beautiful time of the year here in Michigan. Like the grand finale at a display of fireworks, Mother Nature lavishly sends up all her glorious colors in one final and triumphant exhibition before winter sets in with its chilly drabness. The gold, crimson, orange, and red of the maples intermingle with the lemon-yellow of the birches, the rich maroon of the oaks and sumac, and the deep greens of the consistent fir trees to make the landscape one gigantic bouquet. Only a creative God, a powerful, infinite Mind, could conceive such a delightful, variegated riot of color.

God used the same method in creating man. Among the unchanging, immovable phlegmatics, the pines, He put the strong, commanding cholerics, the oaks. Furthermore, to add color to their surroundings, He added the emotional melancholics and sanguines. God created us differently so His work could be accomplished here on earth.

Each individual has physical features which make him easily recognized. Each, also, has an emotional makeup which sets him apart, making him unique.

The men of old—Cain, Abel, Jacob, Esau, Moses,

Aaron, David, Jeremiah, Paul, Peter, Barnabas—possessed varied temperaments. God used all types in the past. He does today.

The role of the emotions and their effect on our lives is a complicated tale, indeed. We bow in awe and humility as we recognize how "fearfully and wonderfully" God has made us. Only a divine imagination could conceive the intricate workings of the human emotions, mind, and body, and their interrelationships.

Our emotions perform various functions. For one thing, they make us more interesting to others. Imagine living with someone who never laughed, cried, or became indignant! What monotony!

Emotions enable us to get more out of life, too. What would life be like without feeling? Emotions cause the Christian to feel the peace, joy, satisfaction, and freedom that Jesus Christ gives.

And our emotions make us act. They arouse response. When our 18-month-old granddaughter came into the living room carrying her three-year-old sister's doll, there was instant emotional reaction. When Christians "feel" concern for others, when they "feel" compelled to witness for the Lord, they begin working for Him. Emotional response produces action.

Human emotions tend to run in cycles. We have both up and down times. Some people will move heaven and earth to carry out their impulses when they are in an elated mood. But when they go into a depression cycle, they are really down-in-the-mouth.

Every pastor, no doubt, encounters those who become enthused periodically. They work "like a house afire" to promote their enthusiasms, but when their emotions wane, they "abandon ship" in a hurry.

It is at the point of the emotions that much discipline is needed. Solomon warned: "He that hath no rule over his own spirit is like a city that is broken down, and without walls" (Prov. 25:28). But, he also said, "He that is slow to anger is better than the mighty; and he that ruleth his spirit than he that taketh a city" (Prov. 16:32).

We are not responsible for our inheritance, emotional or otherwise, but we are accountable for our stewardship. The mature Christian does not act like an uncontrolled child. Disciplining the emotions means "growing in grace." It means to "grow up into him in all things" (Eph. 4:15).

Uncle Buck used to laugh heartily while telling about a fellow churchman.

"Get my name off the book!" the disgruntled member demanded as he stomped out of the church.

"I can't take your name off," Uncle Buck replied, "I haven't a thing to do with it."

"Well, take it off anyway!"

Also, mature Christians do not operate on the basis of feelings. They do what needs to be done whether they feel like it or not.

My husband has preached when he was so ill he had to hold on to the pulpit to give his message to the people.

Many church members have come to prayer meeting when they were so tired they could scarcely drag their feet. But they returned home feeling refreshed and rejuvenated.

Christians who base their claims to salvation on their emotions never progress spiritually. Feelings change and an experience which is dependent on one's emotions will bounce up and down like a rubber ball. God's Word, obedience, and implicit faith form the foundation for building a mature, solid spiritual life in Christ Jesus. It takes a consistent, even walk with God day after day to produce effective witnessing.

The English Quaker, William Penn, said, "No pain, no palm; no thorns, no throne; no gall, no glory; no cross, no crown."

Our emotions can be changed. When going through periods of melancholy, Christians can lift their spirits by contemplating on the bright and cheerful, by finding consolation in God's Word, and by getting involved in helping others.

Maturity calls for the cleansing and empowering help of the Holy Spirit. When we are completely under His control, we are on the road to stability. He can give us the ability to meet adult situations with adult attitudes.

"Happiness is . . . self-control."

Happiness Is . . .

Mental Discipline

I find, by experience, that the mind and the body are more than married, for they are most intimately united; and when the one suffers, the other sympathizes," observed Philip Chesterfield.

Since unhappiness results largely from wrong thinking —worry, fear, insecurity, guilt, and resentment—these undesirables must be replaced with acceptable thoughts if an individual is to enjoy improved health and greater enjoyment.

At this point Christians are often found guilty. Because of the quality of their thinking, they are less than their best for God. Not only do they suffer mentally and physically, but their negative attitudes prevent them from excelling as workers in His vineyard.

Many an earnest Christian finds it difficult to trust the Lord because he has never learned to manage his thought life. He lives beneath his privilege as a child of God, failing to appropriate the faith that would grant him a productive life.

Dwelling on unpleasant subjects, on one's aches and

pains, leads to compounded misery. Thinking about our problems only serves to magnify them.

We must get rid of unwanted, unholy, pessimistic, critical, faithless, negative thoughts by replacing them with loving, virtuous, and positive ones. The person who lives with an "I can" attitude will be more successful than the "I can't" type of individual.

The apostle Paul promised that "the peace of God . . . shall keep your hearts and minds through Christ Jesus." But he went on to urge the Philippians to think on "whatsoever things are true . . . honest . . . just . . . pure . . . lovely . . . of good report."

"If there be any praise," he emphasized, "think on these things" (Phil. 4:7-8).

And Peter advised his readers to "gird up the loins of your mind" (1 Pet. 1:13).

Mental concentration is a valuable exercise. It gives temporary rest to the nerves of the body. Furthermore, when a person becomes absorbed in working a jigsaw puzzle or doing an acrostic, his physical discomforts tend to vanish.

Mental application enables one to get more out of the minister's sermons, the news reports, and recreational reading. It also brings relief for painful self-consciousness.

One lady always looked for something pretty about which to comment. After "Hello" her first words might be, "What a pretty pin you have!" or "What a lovely dress you're wearing!" By concentrating on a previously decided on point, one deflects attention away from oneself.

Disciplined thinking should begin during childhood, but for those who did not learn to curb wandering thoughts in earlier years, hope remains. The ability to concentrate can be strengthened by working puzzles, solving mathematical problems, writing reports, editing manuscripts, and refusing to think about the roast in the oven or tomorrow's dental appointment while the preacher circumnavigates the globe in his pastoral prayer.

We are never too old to stop (or start) learning. Night school classes and correspondence courses provide helpful discipline in the area of mind control.

In *The Disciplined Life*, Richard S. Taylor suggests we practice "thinking in sentences." This tends to bring about orderliness and clarity of thinking.

Learning to concentrate isn't easy for many. Distractions will come. Stray thoughts must be quickly squelched. Without wasting time in regret, however, one must return immediately to the subject. Repeated practice results in habit. And by reducing every good practice to habit that we can, the easier life becomes.

People, especially those troubled by "nerves," are sometimes troubled by compulsive thoughts—ideas or fears which they feel they must hold on to, although they know these thoughts are untrue.

Compulsive thoughts, the result of repressed emotions, stick like burrs in the mind and cause an individual to think them over and over. If a person is to be freed of these undesirables, he must face up to and resolve his inner conflicts.

Quality thinking is also required when it comes to making decisions, something that is especially challenging for overly conscientious people.

Many middle-aged persons still run home to have Mother and Dad make their decisions for them. What a sad day for them when their parents are no longer available!

A mind filled with unsolved problems cannot be at ease. Learning to make decisions as easily and quickly as possible relieves mental tension.

When it comes to making decisions, we have to learn to depend on ourselves, to trust in ourselves. This increases with exercise. We learn to make decisions simply by making them. Here again, daily exercise is a must. "Practice makes perfect." If we make an occasional mistake, so what? Every person does. Through our mistakes we gather experience and gain knowledge and wisdom. On the other hand, by taking note of the times we are successful, our confidence increases.

Reality must be faced—courageously. Difficult problems must be tackled—and solved. Life's obstacles must be wrestled down—and counted out. Jesus faced and won over death. His grace is sufficient. And His wisdom is free for the asking. "If any of you lack wisdom, let him ask of God, that giveth to all men liberally, and upbraideth not; and it shall be given him" (Jas. 1:5).

Before making an important decision, however, one should weigh all sides of the question. It is often wise to consult with knowledgeable persons who may see the problem from different points of view. They may offer new perspectives and valuable suggestions too. It is also wise to compare the problem with similar ones you have experienced in the past.

Having made a decision, we are then ready to move ahead with faith. But we should never forget that some decisions profit by a good night's sleep. Always allow emotions to cool before "stepping on the gas" and moving full speed ahead. Reason and control must not be ditched in one's eagerness to burn up the road with action.

As we are what we eat, so we are what we think. The child who is allowed to do whatever he pleases, minus all restraint, soon becomes discontented and disgruntled. An unbridled mind reacts in much the same way. Thought control is the only means to happiness, for it is through the mind that all impulses, good and bad, enter. Bad thoughts lead to destruction. Good thoughts produce success.

Isaiah promised, "Thou wilt keep him in perfect peace, whose mind is stayed on thee" (Isa. 26:3).

"Happiness is . . . mental discipline."

Happiness Is . . .

Orderliness

A church dignitary told about an assembly he once conducted. The business of the first session was unusually complicated. Delegates made motions. They amended their motions. And then they amended their amendments.

Following the lunch hour, one of the delegates returned to the convention wearing a large button on which were printed the letters B-A-I-K. Naturally the badge attracted attention and aroused curiosity.

"What does B-A-I-K stand for?" someone finally ventured to ask.

"Boy, am I confused!"

"I understand the B stands for boy, A stands for am, I stands for I, but you don't spell confused with a K."

"You don't know how confused I am!" the wearer explained.

A confused mind does not lend itself to happiness. The masses of hurried, disorganized, and anxious beings in today's world prove there is great need for orderliness and poise.

According to Robert Southey, "Order is the sanity of

the mind, the health of the body, the peace of the city, the security of the state. . . . As the beams to a house, as the bones to the body, so is order to all things."

To enjoy health and happiness the mind must be emptied of its clutter and filled instead with positive plans and creative ideas. This is God's will for His children, for He "is not the author of confusion, but of peace" (1 Cor. 14:33).

How does one go about making the transition from chaotic to systematic living?

First, priorities must be recognized and established. What is most important? What needs to be done first? In what order should I tackle the remaining tasks?

"Please tell me how," a parishioner once pleaded. "I work from morning to night. Constantly. And my house looks like this!" Her emaciated frame showed plainly she was not far from collapsing.

When my own children were young, I never seemed to get on top of things either. Finally I decided I needed to get organized. After that, life changed radically—for the better.

For the housewife, simply learning the proper steps to take in cleaning a room—(1) sweep down the walls; (2) wash the woodwork; (3) wash the windows; (4) dust the furniture; (5) polish the windows and glassware; and, (6) vacuum or clean the floors—aids in executing the task with greater ease and more efficiency.

When it comes to general housekeeping, there are a few major tasks which must be done each week—washing, ironing, and cleaning. In between these main chores must be sandwiched many minor ones, such as meal preparations, bed-making, shopping, mending, etc., *ad infinitum.*

If the housewife can set up schedules—one for the week and one for each day—and then stick to them with reasonable constancy, she will find life is much easier on the nerves.

Some overly conscientious Christians have difficulty deciding the relative importance of their responsibilities when it comes to doing "the Lord's work." One housewife spent hours with church interests while her house remained a shambles and her family went uncared for.

Jesus said, "Ye shall be witnesses unto me both in Jerusalem, and in all Judaea, and in Samaria, and unto the uttermost part of the earth" (Acts 1:8). True witnessing begins at home.

It is little wonder a husband loses interest and children run the streets when, day after day, they come home to a wife and mother who is a nervous wreck and a house that looks like the aftermath of a tornado. Failing to keep a proper perspective can make an emotional ruin out of the most pious saint. And misplaced priorities can turn the most religious home into a disaster area.

Despite the worthiness of their execution, the time to roll bandages, prepare posters, and mend clothing for missionary boxes comes after the dishes are washed, the beds are made, the laundry is done, and the beans are boiling for supper. Overly conscientiousness causes some to be tricked by Satan into thinking "good works" must be done even at the expense of home responsibilities.

Solomon said a virtuous woman "looketh well to the ways of her household" (Prov. 31:27). And next to her personal devotion to God, her family's welfare comes next.

Learning to do one thing at a time is a great saver of nervous energy, also. Women who try to cook, sew, and watch rambunctious children simultaneously are bound to end up with a headache, disaster, or probably both.

Then, too, we live with less stress and strain when we avoid striving to hold too many things in our minds. This causes confusion and lessens our efficiency.

I try to keep the many aspects of my busy life in tight compartments—family, church responsibilities, and my writing—with everything sorted out and stored in its proper place.

A calendar keeps notations of appointments and upcoming events. And always there are lists—groceries to be purchased, errands to be run, calls to be made, and letters to be written.

At the beginning of a busy day (or perhaps the night before) I make a list of everything that needs my attention that day. Then I cross the items off as they are cared for. I often do this at the beginning of a week, likewise. That way I am free to take each day as it comes, doing what needs to be done, without worrying about what comes tomorrow. One caution: don't make the day's list unrealistically long.

These reminders take a load off my mind. If I check these lists periodically, I do not have to worry about forgetting or overlooking anything. To paraphrase a popular slogan, "Let your memos do your remembering for you."

Another thing, we need to let our minds "change gears" as we move from one activity to another. This is the day of hurly-burly, excitement, and rush, rush, rush. This is all the more reason, however, to slow down—slow down and live longer. Certainly doing so calls for patience.

Years ago in *Quiet Talks on Personal Problems*, S. D. Gordon wrote: "The other word for unhurriedness is patience. Patience is the most Godlike quality that man can have. It has keen eyes, and quick ears, and a warm heart; it means seeing keenly and feeling deeply and acutely, yet holding still until the fullness of time has come for action."[8]

If we are to enjoy life, we must empty our minds of disorderliness, confusion, and hurry. Mental clutter must go.

"Happiness is . . . orderliness."

Happiness Is . . .

Forgetting

Another practice we must cultivate if we are to enjoy happiness is the ability to forget.

Someone has said, "We must look forward with confidence and courage and backward with no regret."

Jesus said, "No man, having put his hand to the plow, and looking back, is fit for the kingdom of God" (Luke 9:62). The Christian must be a forward thinker. If he allows himself to become depressed, he makes himself vulnerable to the attacks of Satan, who, coward that he is, strikes when we are unable to cope.

I can really become depressed if I dwell on the days when our children were home and we were able to give them little more than the bare necessities of life. If I think about the poor clothes they had to wear, the tough times they had getting through college, my emotions quickly take a plunge.

Our thoughts must not center on past losses, mistakes, failures, sins, hurts, misfortunes, or humiliating experiences. Doing so saps our vitality and prevents us from moving ahead to future accomplishments.

Not a few Christians allow themselves to be tortured by the remembrances of sins they committed in the past and have no way of rectifying. They have deeply repented of their sins and accepted Jesus Christ as their personal Savior, but they cannot forget the past nor forgive themselves.

Divine forgiveness takes care of true guilt, but it never cancels the consequences of past sins. A pregnant girl received forgiveness at an altar of prayer, but she still had to bear the illegitimate child she was carrying.

In *Psycho-Cybernetics*, Dr. Maxwell Maltz points out that by dwelling on our past errors and rebuking ourselves for them, we tend to repeat the very actions we want to change. Recalling those things we should forget serves to enlarge them, and it hinders progress.

One lady was learning to drive. She was so afraid of hitting a certain tree that she watched it too long and ended up doing the very thing she wished to avoid.

Our friend Frank had been a wicked man. The Lord forgave him, but Frank made a bad mistake. He kept repeating stories about his past. Eventually he returned to his evil habits.

Robert Browning reminds us it is good to forgive but best to forget. This applies as well to ourselves as it does to others.

When an individual becomes a child of God, he receives a new set of goals. Thereafter, he must continually "press toward the mark," running the race with patience.

A young woman who had lived a life of deep sinfulness said sorrowfully, "I feel so sad when I think about what my life could have been." I tried to point out to her that she must pick up the reins and "go on from here." She had laid waste much of the past, but she must compensate by making the most of the future.

W. E. Sangster wrote for *Guideposts* some years ago an article entitled "Forget It—and How!" He said we forget by reversing the process of remembering.

To remember, one reviews the image in one's mind,

holds it, then revives it again, repeating the process until the image is fixed in the mind for good.

To forget, one turns the suggestions away from one's mind and substitutes a more acceptable thought or remembrance in its place. For instance, when the memory of a committed sin returns to cause regret and pain, recall, with thanksgiving, the time Christ pardoned you of all your past. When tormented by the recollection of a failure, immediately bring to mind a success you have experienced.

The past can be a tyrant if we let it. But we need not. The apostle Paul said, "This one thing I do, forgetting those things which are behind, and reaching forth unto those things which are before, I press toward the mark" (Phil. 3:13).

The successful, happy Christian looks to the future. His eye is firmly fixed on his goal. While he lives a day at a time here on earth, he also entertains plans and anticipations of things to come. Having something special to look foward to serves to relieve boredom and tension. I am very sure one of the reasons my mother remains youthful is her ability to live expectantly. She is always planning for something. When she hears of an approaching event—a wedding, an anniversary celebration, an expected visitor, the coming of a new baby—she says liltingly, "That will give me something to look forward to."

"I had a pleasant time with my mind, for it was happy," Louisa May Alcott wrote in her *Life, Letters and Journals.*

Just as the mind is where negatives begin and are nurtured, so it is where positive thoughts must be cultivated. Happy thoughts and creative ideas must be tended and coaxed like a gardener treats his prize flowerbeds. Unhappy thoughts and negative suggestions must be weeded out. The soil of our minds must be freed of past stagnations and fertilized with hopes for the future.

"Happiness is . . . forgetting."

Happiness Is . . .

Living Honestly

I hate to look in the mirror, I'm so ugly," I once heard a young lady say. Of course her judgment was prejudiced and faulty. But many people shun really looking at themselves because they do not like what they see within.

Being completely honest is most difficult—for saint and sinner alike. Fear causes people to indulge in dishonesties and untruths (either by omission or commission), or partial truths, in an effort to protect themselves from social pressures. This causes guilt and tension. Sometimes Christians are almost forced into acts of dishonesty—even by well-meaning fellow Christians.

During a church service the evangelist asked, "Will everyone who will win a soul to Christ this year stand up?"

Helen, one of God's truest saints, remained seated. She was aware that others, including her husband, wondered at her refusal to stand. "I know how naturally timid I am," she told me later. "And I seldom get out of the house. It is very unlikely that I will win a soul, so I didn't stand. If the evangelist had asked, 'How many will *try* to win a soul?' I would have stood up."

I admired my friend's honesty and wondered at the times when many of us have rationalized, repressed doubts, or assented to the pressure of the moment and suffered from guilt afterwards. The only way to experience mental health and happiness is to live with ourselves and others honestly. This requires courage, but we all, Christians especially, need to do so.

Although Christians certainly will not deliberately tell falsehoods, many unconsciously defend themselves against failure, disappointment, humiliation, and the woes of life by using less than absolutely straightforward means.

Some always lay the blame on the other fellow. Some protect themselves from frustration by taking out their disagreeable feelings on innocent victims. Rob had had a bad summer. Finally he realized he was holding resentment against his parents because they had prevented him from leading a carefree existence as a child. This caused him to feel edgy and take his misery out on his fiancée, threatening his future.

Many people try to run from the Lord and themselves. Some roam or change jobs too frequently. The beaches and city streets are crowded with unkempt youth attempting to elude responsibility to both God and man. Immature Christians may become church tramps. Some people distract their troubled minds with novels, television, foolish stories, and frivolities.

Unhappiness and dissatisfaction cause others to drown their feelings in overwork. Some keep overly busy—"workaholics"—refusing to take time to relax. On the other hand, sleep can be an escape. While sleeping one is evading frustration, anxiety, and unpleasantness. But sleep does not eliminate problems. They are still present when one awakens.

When threatened by anxiety, some return to earlier ways of acting. A child begins sucking his thumb or talking like a baby. Fearing old age, women may begin dressing like teenagers. Men, fearing loss of virility, may indulge in clandestine escapades. A group of church people may dwell on "the good old days" instead of rolling up their sleeves and going to work on the present situation.

Some protect themselves by taking on the ways of others. Young people "run in packs" as a means of defense. A girl may carry a healthy attitude into marriage if she identifies with a well-adjusted mother, or she may carry a grudge against all men in general if she has "caught" wrong attitudes.

Individuals may suppress disagreeable thoughts by filling their minds with other things. (I had a neighbor who kept her radio, record player, or television running constantly. The noise blocked out her guilt.) All civilized beings must learn to suppress their instinctive urges to an extent, but too much suppression results in dishonest living and produces tension and illness.

Far too many people deal with their anxieties by repressing them or making believe they do not exist. Like a jack-in-the-box, they push the lid down on their anxieties, keeping them below the level of the conscious mind. However, that does not eliminate them. Repression is exhausting to the nervous system. It causes people to live in a perpetual state of confusion. Repressions, however, often erupt in startling and unexpected ways—lapses of memory and slips of the tongue.

Conscious or unconscious illness is often used to "excuse" a person from doing what he doesn't want to do. A headache keeps a child out of school and an adult out of church.

A great number of emotional difficulties and personality upsets are efforts to withdraw from reality. Competition proves too much. If one possesses mediocre or inferior abilities, one may feel unable to cope with life's demands.

Persons may unconsciously seek escape from boredom, humiliation, failure, disappointment, or sustained tension. So called "nervous breakdowns" result.

Christians need to face the facts of reality with faith and courage, resolving their problems as they arise.

Solomon said, "He that covereth his sins shall not prosper" (Prov. 28:13).

Paul wrote, "Pray for us: for we trust we have a good conscience, in all things willing to live honestly" (Heb. 13:18).

Walking humbly with God, keeping an utter submissiveness to His will, and following the admonitions in His Word gives the child of God confidence, inner strength, a sense of well-being, and a mind at ease.

"Happiness is . . . living honestly."

Happiness Is . . .

Living Creatively

Do you remember the happiest moments you spent as a child? Those times probably centered around making mud pies or creating make-believe guns from scrap lumber and rubber-band "bullets" cut from discarded innertubes.

Perhaps playing in mud comes most naturally for children because we're told that "the Lord God formed man of the dust of the ground." But later, He "caused a deep sleep to fall upon Adam, and he slept: and he took one of his ribs . . . and . . . made he a woman" (Gen. 2:7, 21-22).

Because God is creative, and we were made "in his image," we, too, must live creatively if we are to find fulfillment and enjoy happiness.

Since we are individualistic beings, our talents vary. Some have aptitudes for creating delicious cakes, pies, and molded salads. Others design dresses without so much as a pattern. Some can make clocks from discarded bits of equipment. Others construct dune buggies, or erect houses, or paint pictures. Everyone needs a creative outlet. The failure to release pent-up creative tension results in adverse physical conditions.

An imprisoned animal constantly seeks a means of escape. People under tension or stress react much the same way. Some bite their nails. Some eat. Some throw hysterical tantrums. Others twist and squirm, fuss with their clothing, tap their fingers on chairs, count steps, or commit other compulsive acts. These persons should find creative ways of releasing their nervous energy instead of wasting it on useless performances.

It has been observed that "impression without expression results in depression." God has been creating since the beginning of time. We, too, must create or stagnate. Creative expression not only furnishes release for pent-up tension, it also brings fulfillment to the personality, changing gloom to gladness.

Using the imagination keeps life from becoming monotonous, Dr. William Sadler points out in *Theory and Practice of Psychiatry*. Boredom is relieved through the challenge of creative endeavor. What can I make out of this? What can I do with that?

All of life offers opportunity for creativity—cooking, sewing, knitting, homemaking, writing, gardening, painting, landscaping, engineering, preaching, teaching, directing business affairs. The list is endless.

Ilka Chase, best-selling author, once said that her hobby is living and the secret of her enjoyment is creativity.

Every man and woman can develop this ability. Each needs to do so. When a person stops living creatively, he ceases to live enjoyably. Turning *our* disappointments into *His* appointments, our misfortunes into fortunes, and finding good in the not-so-good keeps us alert and alive.

One lady who was suffering from nervous exhaustion read about a person who made crossword puzzles. "I'd like to do that," she decided. After praying about it, she made an attempt. It proved successful; and her desire became a reality.

A minister's wife found her healing through writing. She told me a creative writing course saved her health. "Since my sickness affected my mind (she had hallucinations), I decided that when I got well, I would do something constructive with my mind," she said.

Helen Hunt Jackson was prostrated after the death of her husband. Then she turned to writing and ultimately became a prolific writer, producing many volumes of verse and stories.

"Tell me what you want and I'll fix it," Russ said. This friend of ours, a professional engineer, refuses to discard anything he regards as potentially useful. "Don't throw it away! Maybe I can find a use for it someday," he tells his wife, much to her consternation. However, Russ's junk has a way of becoming attractive and employable articles.

During depression days we were occasionally visited by our city relatives. Their smart attire made us feel more "out of it" than ever. But I learned a lesson from Aunt Ethel which never escaped me. Her example has been a lifetime inspiration.

We listened with amazement and amusement while Aunt Ethel told how she remodeled donated castoffs for her daughters. The garments were ripped apart, washed, pressed, recut, and turned into stylish creations. A worn fur coat became a stunning jacket for one of my cousins. She and her sister were enabled to dress as well as the more affluent because their mother had learned the secret of making something out of next to nothing.

And I have never gotten away from it. "Making something out of nothing" has become a way of life with me. It has helped create interesting homes out of a variety of parsonages. It also enabled us to give two weddings on a shoestring (another story in itself).

"I don't know where you get all your ideas," my mother exclaimed not long ago.

"Whenever I look at anything I ask, 'What can I make out of this?' " I replied. That is why our home is filled with what I call "glorified junk"—odds and ends of furniture, discards, and unlovelies which have been transformed with paint and decals.

Living with imagination is essential for coping with our tensions and relieving monotony. It brings satisfaction for an inborn need. Imagination, a facet of faith, is "the substance of things hoped for," and it, too, is pleasing to God.

"Happiness is . . . living creatively."

Happiness Is . . .

Good Humor

It must be awful having to listen to everyone's complaints," I told our congenial doctor.

"It's better than being a mortician," he replied good-naturedly.

Good humor is necessary for happiness and good health.

"Heaviness in the heart of man maketh it stoop," and "a broken spirit drieth the bones," said Solomon (Prov. 12:25; 17:22). But he also said, "He that is of a merry heart hath a continual feast" (Prov. 15:15).

If anyone has the right to enjoy "a continual feast," it is the Christian. He has received divine forgiveness and freedom from guilt. In Christ he has security, a place of service, peace of mind, and joy unspeakable. Furthermore, he has the hope of eternal life, the promise of heaven to come.

Jesus said, "In the world ye shall have tribulation: but be of good cheer; I have overcome the world" (John 16:33).

Most people are strongly affected by color. Dark, drab, depressing walls, dingy curtains, and faded rugs do not lift the spirits. Bright, gay furnishings exert an uplifting influence. And the same is true of personalities. A cheerful individual can change the atmosphere of his surroundings. He can lift the morale of those with whom he lives and works. He is the redeeming grace of many a home.

Laughter is a wonderful gift of God. A baby smiles before he talks, sits alone, or holds his own bottle. He laughs aloud long before he knows what life is all about, who provides his food, who pays the bills, whom he can trust.

Solomon said, "To every thing there is a season, and a time to every purpose under the heaven . . . a time to laugh" (Eccles. 3:1-4).

A sense of humor dissolves conflict and causes anger to flee. Many household squabbles disappear when doused liberally with laughter and good humor.

Laughter relieves tension and erases strain. Melancholic, serious-minded Abraham Lincoln was saved from despair and the stress he was forced to endure because of his sense of humor. He said, "With the fearful strain that is on me night and day, if I did not laugh I should die."

Perhaps there would be fewer nervous breakdowns in America today if people laughed like we used to laugh during the days of the Depression.

I was raised in a minister's home, the eldest of seven children, when it was a real struggle to make ends meet. My loving father planted potatoes, hung wallpaper, and worked long hours outside the pulpit to provide for us. However low the flour in the barrel, or however worn our shoes, we never lacked for good times. And I shall be eternally grateful because we were taught to live with fun and laughter. Furthermore, I believe it is one of the real reasons all my parents' children are Christians today.

Surely the world would be a nicer place in which to sojourn if more people shared the lighter side of their nature. Can you recall a single person who always displayed a sense of humor or was perpetually cheerful whom you didn't enjoy being around? My brother Fred suffers from a painful back injury but he always is ready to make someone laugh. And people love him.

Our garbage collectors helped make my Christmas jollier one year. Usually their truck was decorated with plastic flowers retrieved from their trash pickups. This year they had secured a wreath to the back of their truck, just above the opening where the garbage was deposited. I hope their sense of the ridiculous brought as much delight to others as it did to me.

And a sense of humor keeps people youthful—"well preserved" instead of "pickled." We cannot stop old age from coming, but blessed are those who remain sweet instead of becoming bitter and sour. As Aunt Grace approached the end of her life, she lost her memory, but one of the few persons she recognized was my father because he had brought so much laughter into her life. Dad and the name of the Lord were among the few bits of recognition she held on to.

Lowell Thomas, network broadcaster, will be remembered not only for his marvelous rich voice and intriguing news stories, but also for his overpowering sense of humor. More than once he burst out laughing while giving the news. Once he inadvertently made a slip of the tongue and it spelled the end of the news for the day. He laughed. And he laughed some more. At last, gasping for breath, he simply gave up with "Oh, my!" His program? Unfinished, but refreshing.

Bill D. Moyers, press secretary to President Lyndon Johnson, turned his job over to George Christian with this advice: "Work hard and keep your sense of humor."

Perhaps that is good advice for all of us. Many of us,

born-again Christians included, should stop being so touchy. At least we could learn to laugh at ourselves, if at nothing else. If we can do that, we need never worry about running out of amusement.

"Happiness is . . . good humor."

Happiness Is . . .

Giving a Smile

There is no happiness in having or in getting, but only in giving," said Henry Drummond.

A talented young man had just presented an outstanding instrumental number. His singular rendition brought expressions of delight from the audience. With the others, his bride, radiant and charming, had given him her rapt attention and admiration. Then came a voice from behind.

"And to think," someone said, "all his wife can do is smile!"

Certainly the careless speaker did not realize his stinging remark would send the new wife home with a broken heart. He did not know the feeling of inadequacy she suffered because of her own lack of musical talent. Nor did he realize how mistaken he was in disparaging her ability to give cheerful smiles easily and liberally.

Someone has said that although a smile doesn't cost a cent, it is worth a million dollars. Smiles, many times, are worth more than great talent. The young lady would not have wept so bitterly if she had realized how richly she had been endowed. And if the young man who sat behind her had been more knowledgeable, he would not have spoken so thoughtlessly.

Henry Ward Beecher said: "Nothing on earth can smile but man! Gems may flash reflected light, but what is a diamond flash compared with an eye-flash or a mirth-flash? Flowers cannot smile; this is a charm that even they cannot claim. It is a light in the windows of the face, by which the heart signifies it is at home and waiting. A face that cannot smile is like a bud that cannot blossom and dries up on the stalk. Laughter is day, and sobriety is night, and a smile is the twilight that hovers gently between—more bewitching than either."

It costs nothing in dollars and cents to give a smile, but the memory of a smile can last forever. When one is depressed and life has lost its glow, a smile given by another can be a never-forgotten experience.

One of the best ways to acquire friends is to learn to smile. However, a smile must come from the heart. The mechanical kind will not suffice. The world nowadays is overrun with commercials in which models exhibit the false kind. A real smile must radiate true friendliness. One must love people. Before one can truly love others, one must be endued with the love of God.

A smile knows no barriers. It means the same in any language. Anyone can understand a smile.

It has been asserted by a well-regarded psychologist that smiling is relaxing. In this day of tension we need to relax more often. Relaxation benefits the nerves, thus easing physical ills.

People who have the ability to smile seldom have trouble obtaining work. They are nice to be around. They help the morale of those with whom they associate. It isn't so difficult to go to work in the morning if someone is there to greet you with a smile instead of a disgruntled moan. The boss prospers and is benefited by employees who are cheerful and optimistic. Workers accomplish more in pleasant surroundings.

Down through the years I have become a Jill-of-all-trades. Being a minister's wife, this is a necessity. One Sunday morning when I was ill and unable to attend services, I indulged in a bit of self-pity. What will they miss today— my piano playing, my teaching, my singing? I wondered.

A few days later one of the ladies told me, "My sister and I were talking about your absence Sunday. Oh, how we missed your smile!"

Even though I was a bit taken back at the time, I have come to recognize those words as a real compliment. To be able to smile has its compensations. It automatically designates you as a friendly person. It marks you as being cheerful and kind, a nice person to be near. Smiles melt away icy barriers. They thaw out cold personalities and help feelings of envy and jealousy to disappear.

So if God endowed you with an automatic smile, be truly grateful. If not, learn the art. Begin today. Let the love of God warm your own heart until you feel love for all mankind. Once He fills your heart to overflowing, never let it stop. Go right on being a "bottle of sunshine" to all you meet.

It isn't always easy to smile even if you are one of those who seem to smile automatically. Sometimes clouds overshadow our horizons. It has been noted that when everything is going smoothly, most anyone can smile, but when adversities beset us, it takes a valiant person to do so.

Don't be discouraged if you meet a person who is too busy, or preoccupied, or disgruntled to smile. Smile anyway. Who needs it worse than he?

And don't be stingy! Be lavish with your smiles. The world is starving for them. There is no overabundance anywhere. Nor will there be.

The more I think about the young bride and the care-

less youth, the less I feel sorry for her and the more I pity
him. He has a lot to learn. Talents are wonderful and not to
be discredited, but the heart that has learned to smile has
really arrived.

King Solomon observed that "a merry heart maketh a
cheerful countenance" (Prov. 15:13); and, "a merry heart
doeth good like a medicine" (17:22).

Someone observed that a person must wear a smile to be
properly clothed. Before appearing in public, we give care-
ful attention to our hairdo and the details of our dress. Let
us remember to check on the most important item of all—
the expression we wear on our face.

"Happiness is . . . giving a smile."

Happiness Is . . . .

Simplicity

The greatest truths are the simplest; and so are the greatest men," said August W. Hare.

Ralph Waldo Emerson observed: "Nothing is more simple than greatness; indeed, to be simple is to be great."

It is always refreshing to see simplicity displayed in the lives of the famous. More than 100 presidents, kings, and prime ministers attended the funeral of Charles De Gaulle in the Notre Dame Cathedral in Paris, France. But at his request the great general was buried with unusual simplicity. He was laid to rest in a simple oaken coffin in his own village, among the common people he loved.

Simplicity is required of all of God's family, for only as we become as little children can we enter into His kingdom (Luke 18:17). The Heavenly Father has hidden many things from the wise and prodent but revealed them, Jesus said, "unto babes" (Matt. 11:25).

Jesus himself used simple, down-to-earth, everyday stories to captivate His audiences, and "the common people heard him gladly" (Mark 12:37). His illustrations were from the common experiences of life.

As soldiers in the army of the Lord, we do well to heed

Paul's advice to Timothy: "No man that warreth entangleth himself with the affairs of this life" (2 Tim. 2:4).

The ability to derive satisfaction from simple, everyday pleasures is one of the characteristics of mental health. Enjoying a sunrise or sunset, the smile of a baby, the antics of children, the variety of the seasons, a meal of corn bread and milk or a bowl of rice can produce far greater happiness than the luxuries which are dependent on wealth and affluence.

Eliminating the superfluous lessens tension, the creator of "nerves." Often our lives become overcharged or cluttered with nonessentials. Many could be profitably and easily excluded.

Henry David Thoreau believed "our life is frittered away by detail," and he urged, "Simplify, simplify."

In an age when so many of our youth feel they must begin married life with everything Mom and Dad possess after 30 years' accumulation, the recent experiences of Dan and Dale intrigued me. With a maturity that is rare for young people these days, they found happiness in living simply and creatively.

Both came from less than affluent parentage. Both obtained a college education without the benefit of liberal allowances. However, the fact that their happiness increases with the passing years proves something of value. A life of ease and permissiveness does not guarantee satisfaction. Learning to live contentedly with less while young may serve to increase one's enjoyment during the later years of life.

Getting through college on a shoestring was more pleasure than pain for Dale, an able seamstress and home economics major. With deft and capable fingers she economically created not only her college wardrobes but also her bridal gown and the dresses for her attendants.

Married immediately following their graduation from

college, Dan and Dale spent their honeymoon traveling from her home in North Dakota to the rural church in northern Michigan that Dan was to pastor for the next few years.

While her new husband preached, visited, counseled, and administered, Dale taught school, continued to make her own dresses from materials obtained on sales counters, and economize through various ingenious means. When, at last, Dan decided to attend seminary, they were able to make the move and purchase a modest little home in the distant city.

Having used the major portion of their savings for a down payment on their house, the next question was how to furnish their nest. But the challenge was of little consequence to a couple like Dan and Dale. They decided to play it smart. Instead of going into debt to impress their acquaintances, they chose to furnish their home with bargains obtained at garage and house sales. And they enjoyed every minute of it.

There were many things to learn—some at considerable expense to their ingenuity—but they made both the good and bad of their experiences into something like a circus. More than once they were tempted to feel they had made monkeys of themselves, but the end result of their escapades was elephant-sized compensation.

Before Dan's stint in seminary was over, he sought for further means of conserving expense. This he did by purchasing a motorcycle to ride to and from school and his part-time job. It proved so rewarding and fascinating that he was soon able to convince Dale to ride too. The climax came one summer when they returned to Michigan from Missouri to visit. Their mode of travel—800 miles on their motorcycle—accompanied by laughter, intrigue, and a few muscular aches and pains.

Always Dale's ingenuity came through. While in seminary they assisted in a church some distance from their home. Sometimes they drove their car. Often they hopped on their motorcycle to make the considerable journey. Dale managed with a matching three-piece outfit, changing her slacks for the skirt upon their arrival.

Now that their education has been completed, it will be interesting to follow the shenanigans of these two in the full-time pastorate. One thing is for sure: life will not be boring nor monotonous. Nor unhappy.

If you need to unload the surplus baggage from your daily living, you can begin by taking a realistic look at your surroundings. Has your existence become encumbered with superfluous accumulations of one kind and another? What can be eliminated—materially and time-wise? What is truly important? What is of no true consequence? Could it be dropped? With modern-day materials and conveniences, we can find ways to cut down on wasted time, time that could be put to better advantage.

Why wash, starch, and iron doilies when bare-topped tables are popular and attractive? Or, plastic doilies will substitute as nicely? Why not remove unnecessary knick-knacks and save hours of dusting (which might be used more profitably in prayer, Bible study, and witnessing)? The barer a house is, the cleaner it looks. Why not replace ruffled curtains with easy-to-care-for draperies?

Men, too, can become overly encumbered with non-essentials. One fellow I know keeps so busy painting and repainting his buildings, meticulously caring for his lawn and garden that he never takes time to "get away from it all."

It is easy for a Christian to "take on" more than he can reasonably handle—especially if he is conscientious. Although the vast majority flee from Kingdom responsibilities, yet occasionally we find an individual who assumes so many church jobs that he is unable to do justice to any of them.

Not a few eager, conscientious souls "ask" for jobs, or accept them enthusiastically, only to throw up their hands in defeat shortly. It would be better to limit themselves to one or two tasks and then faithfully execute them without suffering from tension. And causing their families to "pay" for it, too. (Isn't it sad that the zealousness of churchmen is so often unevenly distributed?)

Living with fewer complications can help bring us into a closer relationship with the Father in heaven. Keeping life simpler allows time for becoming better acquainted with Him. Bondage to temporal things prevents spiritual growth and adventure. Keeping a loose hold on earth's treasures heightens the anticipation of heavenly store. After all, the Lord packed no bag and sent no luggage with us when we made our earthly debut; and He has ordained that we shall take nothing with us when we make our demise.

"Happiness is . . . simplicity."

Happiness Is . . .

Contentment

Charles Farrar Browne said facetiously: "Let us all be happy and live within our means, even if we have to borrow the money to do it with."

Not too long ago someone asked me, "What do you do to feel bubbly on the inside?"

Now that is a difficult question to answer. Happiness involves many things. Knowing Christ in an intimate way is the first requisite. Inner conflicts—guilts, worries, fears, and resentments—must be resolved. Added to that, one must learn to be contented with his state of life. Or set about to change it.

The apostle Paul was troubled, distressed, perplexed, but he was not in despair. He was "persecuted, but not forsaken; cast down, but not destroyed" (2 Cor. 4:9). What was Paul's secret? Why was he never frustrated to the point of despair? Why could he live in hope?

For one thing Paul avoided discontentment. He testified, "I have learned in whatsoever state I am, therewith to be content" (Phil. 4:11). He recognized that "godliness with contentment is great gain." He reminded Timothy, "We brought nothing into this world, and it is certain we can carry nothing out. . . . Having food and raiment let us be . . . content" (1 Tim. 6:6-8).

The missionary-apostle warned that the rich fall into temptations, snares, and hurtful lusts, and that "the love of money is the root of all evil" (1 Tim. 6:10).

An article in *Woman's Day* stated that men wish their wives to be happy. Discontentment and fretfulness kill many loves. When a woman lets her husband know she is happy to be living with him, it gives him the confidence to go out and whip the world.

I heard a distinguished minister comment on the fact that the Israelites almost gave up the Promised Land because they had no leeks and garlic. Moses had to get God's people out of Egypt; and then, he had to get Egypt out of them. Imagine exchanging heavenly manna for onions! That is what discontentment will do.

Solomon certainly must have been an authority on women. At least he had plenty of opportunity to know their ways and wiles. (Whether he ever came to understand them is another matter.) "Better is a dry morsel, and quietness therewith, than an house full of sacrifice with strife," he said (Prov. 17:1).

"A perverse temper, and a discontented, fretful disposition, wherever they prevail, render any state of life unhappy," said Cicero, the Roman orator.

Another early Roman, Horace, said, "You traverse the world in search of happiness, which is within the reach of every man; a contented mind confers it all."

Marcus Aurelius Antoninus, who lived during the second century following Christ, cautioned, "Remember this, that very little is needed to make a happy life."

Socrates, the Greek philosopher, declared, "He is richest who is content with the least, for content is the wealth of nature."

And Charles Spurgeon, the oft-quoted English clergyman of the 19th century, said, "It is not how much we have, but how much we enjoy, that makes happiness."

Contentment is a state of mind. It is not procured through the accumulation of things. Carpeted floors, stereos, television sets, sterling, china, and lavish yachts do not bring it. Some of the wealthiest, plushest homes are as cold as chilled clabber. They are filled with countless appliances, luxuries, and objets d'art, but love has been pushed out. Only the shell, the pretense, of a home remains.

It was with this vein of thought in mind some years back that I wrote the following lines:

Until now this has been more or less of a personal thing. But perhaps the time has come to share my secret with the world.

It's a game I have been playing for years which will save any conscientious player hundreds of dollars.

I was brought up in a minister's home during the depression—a compound fracture, to say the least. My husband and I were married when we were penniless kids. Then a few years later, the Lord called him to preach. Needless to say, I have lived on a limited budget all my life.

So, of necessity, I have learned to live happily without many things. But it is *the* game that has taken the ouch out of my restricted spending. Anyone can play it. And you need no expensive toggery or special equipment.

It goes like this. Walk into a store. Stroll up and down the aisles. Find something that is attractive to you. Look at it carefully. Admire it. Drool a bit. Admit you would like to have it. "Yes, I surely would," you say with feeling.

Then . . . this is where the game becomes effective. You use your logic and willpower, not your emotions. Look at the object again honestly. As objectively as you can, ask yourself the following questions: Do I really need this? Can I live without it? Do I have to have it?

If you are absolutely honest (and you must be if you

play the game well), 99 times out of 100 you'll put the coveted item back on the shelf, heave a sigh of relief, and push your cart down the supermarket aisle.

"Of course I can get along without that!" you add triumphantly.

Now this is where the fun comes in. Down deep inside you feel just wonderful. You have heeded Paul's advice to beware of covetousness, and you have won a victory over the wasteful practice of accumulating "things."

When Paul said, "My God shall supply all your need," he did not promise that God would give us everything we are tempted to purchase. And let's face it: We can live without much more than we are prone to believe we can.

Covetousness is a modern-day sickness which has brought spiritual death to many Christians. It is something we must guard against lest we be caught in its viselike grasp.

Knicknacks, electric gadgets, automatic appliances, ornaments, expensive entertainment, snowmobiles, and lake cruisers are nice—if we can afford them. But many one-time ardent church workers have gone on spending sprees until they had to hold down two or three jobs in order to meet their monthly "easy" installment plan payments. In doing so, they are keeping their children out of Sunday school, missing out on church services—Sunday and mid-week—and failing to find time to read the Bible and pray. They are losing their souls over "things."

When the Lord calls us home, we must leave empty-handed. We cannot take one electric or automatic gadget with us. Every material item we possess must remain behind.

Is it worth it? Does it pay to load oneself down with financial worries until one is filled with anxiety and robbed of peace and joy? Does it pay to exchange eternal salvation for temporal satisfaction?

As for me, I plan to go on playing my game. It works

wonders. I have found I can get along without many things. It has saved me hundreds of dollars and, for a fringe benefit, I have peace of mind and soul.

John Stuart Mill said, "I have learned to seek my happiness by limiting my desires, rather than in attempting to satisfy them."

I agree. "Happiness is . . . contentment."

Happiness Is . . .

A Grateful Heart

Two-year-old Shari, her parents, and baby sister were traveling "over the hills and through the cities" to spend Thanksgiving Day with us. Shari, fastened securely in a seat belt in the back seat, sang happily, "Thank You, Lord, for restaurants."

Have you ever thanked the Lord for a restaurant? I'm sure I have while traveling, but so often we fail to thank Him for the ordinary, commonplace things in life. Sometimes it takes a little child to remind us that His praises should continually be in our mouths. Not just at this special season of the year, but moment by moment, day in and day out, year after year.

Maeterlinck pointed out that happiness is rarely absent in our lives, but we fail to recognize its presence. One way to know if you're happy or not is to count your blessings. When you begin enumerating everything the Lord has given you, it isn't long until your emotions have changed radically.

Thomas Secker said, "A grateful mind is both a great and a happy mind."

If we modern-day housewives are tempted to complain over trivia, we need to frequently read this excerpt taken from Granny Bee Bee's diary. It is one of my favorite clippings:

RECEET FOR WASHING CLOTHES

1. Bild fire in back yard, to het kettle of rain water.
2. Set tubs so smoke wont blow in eyes, if wind is pert.
3. Shave one hole cake lie sope in bilin water.
4. Sort things, make 3 piles, 1 pile white, 1 pile cullard, 1 pile work britches and rags.
5. Stur flour in cold water to smooth, then thin down with bilin water.
6. Rub dirty spots on board, scrub hard, then bile.
7. Rub cullard, but don't bile, just rench and starch.
8. Take white things out of kettle with broom stick handel, then rench, blew and starch.
9. Spread tee towels on grass.
10. Hang old rags and britches on fence.
11. Por rench water in flower bed.
12. Scrub porch with hot soapy water.
13. Turn tubs up side down.
14. Go put on clean dress, smooth hair with side combs, brew a cup of tee, set and rest and rock a spell, and count your blessings.

One day we called on an elderly couple who at that time had been married 58 years. He was an invalid. She got around the house with the aid of a walker. Neither was able to leave the house. "Oh, sometimes I get discouraged," she said, "but then I begin to think of all the things we have to be thankful for—we have enough to eat, we're warm, we can hear, we can see." She added cheerfully, "Then I feel better. People have a lot to be thankful for."

Occasionally I have made a special effort to thank the Lord for the many material blessings He has bestowed on my husband and me since we were married by recalling our first home, scantily furnished, mostly with borrowed furniture at that. As I've looked about the rooms of our present home, I've thanked Him for the many items, one by one, that we have accumulated since those lean depression years. And my heart has welled with gratitude. Truly He has been wonderful to us . . . and to our children. And I cannot help exclaiming with the Psalmist, "Blessed be the Lord, who daily loadeth us with benefits" (Ps. 68:19).

But the apostle Paul reminds us that we are to give "thanks always for all things" (Eph. 5:20). It isn't difficult to say "Thank You, Lord" for the good things that happen to us, but it is sometimes more challenging to feel grateful for frustrations and hardships. Nevertheless, as His children we must recognize that God is in all He allows to come to us.

"It's marvelous how the Lord worked," I've heard my friend Ellie say many times, despite much physical suffering.

The social secretary at the White House was asked in an interview what advice she would give to her successor. She replied, "Enjoy every minute of it—even the frustrations."

Blessings can come even from our failures and frustrations if we look for them. Times of suffering and hardship can create precious memories. Remember when the children were still under feet? (My mother declares they were the happiest days of her life.) You wondered how you would buy more shoes and pay the grocery and doctor bills. When the baby cried, the older children fussed, the water pipes froze, you didn't know what to do first. Now the children are grown and gone and you look back on those times with yearning and nostalgia.

Even troubles can produce happiness if we take a creative attitude toward them. God often teaches us our most precious lessons during periods of adversity. And failures cause us to look for new and better ways of doing things, thus increasing our effectiveness.

Praise opens the door to God's presence. As we express our appreciation to Him and assure Him of our devotion,

His great heart is warmed and He warms our own hearts in
return. Yes, "it is a good thing to give thanks unto the Lord"
(Ps. 92:1).

"Happiness is . . . a grateful heart."

Happiness Is . . .

Enjoying Your Work

Letitia Elizabeth Landon, an English poetess of the 19th century, said, "No thoroughly occupied man was ever yet very miserable."

It's a tremendous experience to find yourself doing exactly what you want to do. I can truthfully say this is my status in life. I love being my husband's wife. I love being a mother. A grandmother. A minister's wife. A writer.

Life is just right for me!

Many people are not as fortunate as I. Some are trying to do that for which they are unsuited. This causes unhappiness and often, failure. Every individual needs to enjoy his life's work, letting it serve as a means of self-expression. Work that is fitted to one's personality, aptitudes, dreams, and ambitions brings fulfillment.

Dr. George S. Stevenson has said that a sign of mental health is the ability to put your best efforts into what you do and derive satisfaction out of it. Work is not only a necessity, but it can be therapeutic.

William Feather said he had observed people in all walks of life and he could not recall one thoroughly good workman who was a thoroughly unhappy man.

In discussing the drug problem, a psychiatrist at a state hospital, with more than two score years of practice and a broad experience with drug-using teen-agers, said, "You've got to keep them busy. Many of them are highly intelligent and basically creative children. So you present them with creative tasks to perform. You have to build their ego."

Remember the old adage, "The idle mind is the devil's workshop"? My father knew that work remedied that situation. It is unfortunate for many other people that their parents did not recognize this truth. By trying to spare their children, they caused them to suffer fom other pains, pains caused by worry, self-concern, and self-centeredness. Individuals with time on their hands (and minds) are more apt to be sick than those who have no opportunity to pamper themselves.

George Sand said, "Work is not man's punishment. It is his reward and his strength, his glory and his pleasure."

Golda Meir, former prime minister of Israel, migrated to the United States from Russia with her parents and sisters when she was a young girl. To earn a living the family had to work extremely long hours. "I was never given an opportunity to be spoiled by leisure," said the lady who came to be called "Israel's Tough Grandmother-Prime Minister."

Work which requires exercise offers release for built-up tension and pent-up emotions. A punching bag affords an outlet for anger and resentment, but a lawnmower, a hoe, or a scrub brush do also—with profit.

Inadequate exercise can result in jangled nerves, disordered digestion, a sluggish liver, and nervous collapse. Exercise works off the poisons which are imprisoned in the system. This should be good news for women who do their own housework!

"Men in sedentary jobs store their tensions," said Dr. Fred Kasch. So never feel sorry for the man who must mow the lawn or help his wife with the heavier household tasks after office working hours are over.

According to another doctor, hykinesis is a lack of body movement. Its symptoms are overweight, fatigue, depression, irritability, and sleeplessness. The cure is exercise.

At a mental hospital where Vivian was recovering, she was given work to do in the sewing room. Although making apron strings would not appeal to most of us, Vivian told me, "It's kinda' fun."

In *Who Walk Alone*, Peggy Burgess wrote about an American soldier who served in the Spanish-American War. Nine years after returning home, "Ned Langford" discovered he had contracted leprosy. Probably no other individual can imagine the mental suffering "Ned" endured, unless he has experienced it. After passing through seasons of terrified acceptance, hellish despair, and finally, apathetic resignation, "Ned" found healing through work. He helped himself by helping other victims of leprosy.

An article written by Mary McSherry, entitled "Why Some Men Live Longer," appeared in the October, 1971, *Woman's Day*. It told about a study made by a 19-man team from Harvard's School of Public Health and the School of Medicine at Trinity College in Dublin, Ireland. These men compared 575 pairs of brothers born in Ireland, with one remaining on his native soil while the other half of each pair migrated to America. Those who became Americans had more heart disease than their blood relatives in Ireland. The study concluded that the difference in health status was largely due to less stress and more physical activity on the part of the brothers who stayed in Ireland. They worked harder but lived longer.[9]

However, satisfying work still calls for caution. The Christian life demands discipline in every area. One minister kept so busy with "good" things that his family began secretly removing the telephone receiver from the hook in an effort to restrain him from leaving the house. At last, his own child turned against him because of his neglect where his family was concerned.

Before writing *Rx for "Nerves,"* I asked the president of a Christian college about the problem of tension which is affecting so many Christians today. What did he think was the cause? He replied that he thought we demand too much of ourselves. We push when we should stop pushing. We work when we should rest from work. "I find myself working seven days a week if I don't watch it," he said.

I also asked an influential clergyman his opinion. He thought it was not overwork but worry over work that was to blame.

S. D. Gordon wrote: "A great deal of worry is wholly due to physical causes. Overworked nerves always see things distorted. Huge, phantom shapes loom up before us. Overwork always makes a sensitive spirit worry, and worry usually makes us overwork until we drop from exhaustion."[10]

This, of course, reminds one of the age-old question: "Which came first, the chicken or the egg?" Who can say which is the true answer? People definitely react in diverse ways. One remains "cool, calm, and collected" while another "goes bananas." So long as we live in earthen vessels, we shall be subjected to stress, but most of us can learn to live with far less then we do.

Naturally, the worker who punches the time clock without a second to spare, out of breath and head in a whirl, is destined to suffer from stress. And his employer can expect inferior workmanship.

But by rising promptly, perhaps a bit earlier than necessary (or staying awake when the alarm rings instead of catching 10 extra winks), by dressing immediately, enjoying a time of devotion with the Lord, and getting to work a few minutes ahead of schedule, a worker can begin the day with a calm mind and steady nerves.

Likewise, the nervous individual should train himself to think before he acts. When a fellow worker or member of the family calls for attention, he should avoid jumping out of his skin. Instead, he should strive to remain cool by taking deliberate action to do so, thinking first, then acting. Such practice can reverse a habit.

"God is unhurried. He is keenly watching; never indifferent. He is accurate; never missing the mark of His purpose. He is prompt; never ahead of time, and never late. Man was made in the image of God," writes S. D. Gordon.[11]

Fulfilling, satisfying, and rewarding work is still God's plan for man. Solomon said, "In all labour there is profit" (Prov. 14:23).

We should avoid tackling our tasks with a sledgehammer or wrecking-bar tenacity. Contrarily, we should seek to work with ease and skill, with efficiency and pride, and derive satisfaction from jobs well done.

"Happiness is . . . enjoying your work."

Happiness Is . . .

Relaxing with a Hobby

Living for the Lord gives the Christian purpose. Doing all for the love of Jesus adds luster to his life. Suitable work brings fulfillment. But every person also profits from recreation.

Because the Christian is human, he occasionally needs to rest his mind and body from his everyday routine. Relaxation must follow periods of tension. Work, play, exercise, and rest must be kept in proper proportions if one is to enjoy health and happiness.

Someone has said, "Choose such pleasures as recreate much and cost little."

Individuals who engage in strenuous mental work especially need to divert their attention from their work periodically. Solomon knew this, for he said, "Much study is a weariness to the flesh" (Eccles. 12:12).

Phoedrus observed: "The mind ought sometimes to be diverted that it may return to better thinking."

We all profit from a yearly vacation. A change of scenery and environment does us good. We come home (or go back to work) feeling refreshed and ready to tackle our tasks with new zeal and enthusiasm.

A vacation is one which gives a complete change in tempo and viewpoint. For that reason people who live in the city find rest visiting the country and rural persons find diversion visiting the city.

"Mini" vacations also serve to relieve tension and fatigue. We can take these often—perhaps daily—by pursuing diversified interests, recreations, hobbies, and creative endeavors.

The reason Dr. Albert Schweitzer, theologian, musician, physician, and administrator, could accomplish all he did was due to the fact that he changed frequently from one activity to another.

Too often we humans keep driving until we exhaust our mental and physical strength. Suffering from a bout of exhaustion, I visited the doctor.

The poor man had prescribed and diagnosed until he was in a quandary. Finally he asked, "Don't you ever do anything you like to do?"

If people would learn to take more time for mini-vacations, or hobbies, they would actually accomplish more in the long run, for a change of activity renews and revitalizes one's spirit and brings new vigor and enthusiasm.

Margot told me how she overcame a seige of "nerves" following the death of her husband. "I did exactly what I felt like doing," she said. "If I felt the urge to paint the furniture, I painted the furniture." By disregarding her normal routine and indulging in mind-changing endeavor, she regained her health and strength.

After the children leave home, women, especially, are adversely affected. They tend to feel that life is over, that they are not needed anymore. It is then they need to devote themselves to developing new interests.

Becoming involved with soul-winning and other church activities offers a wonderful outlet for Christians. Acceptable secular interests may afford further relaxation. Joining a bowling team or a painting class may bring rejuvenation. The individual who has several interests finds it still easier to avoid monotony. If one enjoys teaching a Sunday school class, rolling bandages for medical mission work, listening to good music, reading, swimming, golfing, and antiquing, there is always something to offer a change of mind and activity. While too many interests may be self-defeating, several real ones are ncecessary for a full and enjoyable life.

Keeping active is also the key to growing old gracefully. Pursuing hobbies and recreations keeps people from becoming self-centered and preoccupied with themselves. Outside interests add zest to living. Being involved with others keeps an individual vibrant and alert.

Our friend, Rev. W. W. Clay, pastored churches until he was in his mid-80s. My parents thoroughly enjoyed a trip to the Holy Land when both were nearing the four score mark.

Enjoying a hobby brings relief for times of frustration. When our girls were growing up, it amused us to see them sometimes laughingly scream into a pillow to vent some frustration. Hobbies afford a more acceptable outlet for pent-up "steam," or tension.

David, our son-in-law, relaxes from his schoolteaching stints by operating miniature trains. Jerry, a real estate broker, dons work clothes and does manual labor.

The list is endless. From the most demanding sports to the quietest kind of activity, everyone can find fulfillment for his need for relaxation. For this reason, the value of creative hobbies cannot be overestimated.

Michelangelo said, "It is only well with me when I have a chisel in my hand."

Johann von Goethe said, "The man who is born with a talent which he is meant to use finds his greatest happiness in using it."

"I get lost when I make fur hats," a milliner told me.

Another lady "forgets everything" when she works jigsaw puzzles.

Reading is still a profitable pastime and by using the facilities of our libraries, it is practically expense-free. People who enjoy books, magazines, and papers are continually receiving new ideas. Living imaginatively is insurance against boredom.

Furthermore, reading brings one a better understanding of oneself. And it increases self-confidence. When we discover others have experienced our same thoughts and feelings, we decide we are not so "far out" as we thought.

Reading helps one forget one's troubles also. While living temporarily in the world of Paul the apostle, Jane Eyre, David Copperfield, Huckleberry Finn, Lowell Thomas, or *The Old Man and the Sea*, one forgets one's worries and fatigue.

Our feelings change as our ideas change. A baby can be in tears until his attention is diverted to an amusing toy. Then he stops crying and laughs instead. An interesting novel or a game of bowling may do the same for an adult.

Among his rules for enjoying happiness, Grenville Kleiser urged having a hobby—an avocation which brings diversion and relaxation. It improves both mental and physical health.

"Happiness is . . . relaxing with a hobby."

Happiness Is . . .

Self-forgetfulness

Where do you draw the line?" someone once asked me. "Just how much attention should you give to yourself and how much should you give to others?"

If I had to take a chance on overdoing one, I would rather be found "going overboard" for others than to be guilty of self-centeredness. Wouldn't you?

Jesus said, "If any man will come after me, let him deny himself . . . for whosoever will save his life shall lose it: and whosoever will lose his life for my sake shall find it" (Matt. 16:24-25).

Self-forgetfulness is a necessity if we want to enjoy mental health and happiness. Happiness comes through sharing, and this the self-centered person does not do. He is so involved with his own fatigue, aches, and pains, he cannot listen to the concerns of others.

Nor can he see himself as others see him. He may wonder why people don't care to be around him, why he isn't as popular as he would like to be. He needs to realize that people want to be around those who are happy, those who make them feel better, those who have something to give.

But the self-centered individual does not give. He is too busy seeking understanding and sympathy for himself. He has no time to "put himself out" for someone else. Even those nearest and dearest to him are forced to suffer because of his self-interest.

The way out of self-centeredness is not easy. Stopford A. Brooke said:

> It is hard, when we are the victims of feelings which eat at our heart day and night, to force ourselves into the life of giving, of doing little things for others, or stepping out of our reserve, of conquering our wish for solitude, of going to cheer and comfort those who are dependent upon us, of surrendering our pride, of doing a little good here and there when we had rather do big things; but it is the true way to get rid of the enslaving dominion of the greater passions.
>
> It will bring peace at last, for it is at the root of God's peace. It was the calm of Christ, and when He left us His last legacy of peace He left the means of it in the New Commandment: "Love one another as I have loved you."[12]

Self-forgetfulness is a way of life to be cultivated. Many self-centered individuals look covetously at their outgoing neighbors. They yearn to experience the same happiness. And they can—if they are willing to work at the job, to pay the price. Like trying to conquer any habit, turning from self-interest is difficult to do. But it can be done through prayer and persistent effort.

Dr. William Sadler maintains that people must learn to live in such a manner that they keep their minds off themselves.[13]

Grenville Kleiser observed that we experience happiness in proportion to the degree we give, serve, and help others.

Self-forgetfulness is the secret of overcoming painful self-consciousness, which is in reality, selfishness. Someone has said that the self-conscious person has his ego in the forefront of his attention. This is why he must turn his attention away from self to others.

Self-consciousness is a maladjustment which has its beginning early in life when the attention of others is focused on us. Therefore, we are not at fault for its inception, but we can help ourselves overcome it by turning outward, pursuing worthy causes, winning souls to Christ, comforting the lonely, and looking for ways to lighten the burdens of others.

A dynamic missionary to Africa said, "Self-pity is poison." If you are tempted to feel sorry for yourself, begin observing those around you. There are thousands far worse off than you and I. For instance, we visited with a lady in a hospital who had had both legs amputated. Awaiting an uncertain future, she continued to scatter sunshine. As we left her room, our own hearts were warmed and cheered.

There is no excuse for resorting to self-pity when there are so many in real need. Worthwhile service to others yields big dividends. When we are busy doing something for someone who is worse off than we are, our own misery is eclipsed.

Individuals who are troubled by "nerves" often seek to be alone—which is exactly what they should *not* do. We all need times of quietness and solitude in order to meditate, pray, and organize our thoughts, but for the "ingrown" person, these times should be limited.

Associating with others is sometimes costly. It is not always easy to put up with the faults and demands of other people, but the price a person pays if he shuns the association of others is greater. Therefore, he must learn to be tolerant—to give cheerfully, put up with the weaknesses of the less fortunate, and respect the rights of his associates. To grow out of self-centeredness, one should seek out and find as many to help as possible. Jane Porter said, "Happiness is not perfected until it is shared."

Jesus said, "He that loseth his life for my sake shall find it" (Matt. 11:39).

"Happiness is . . . self-forgetfulness."

Happiness Is . . .

Loving

The telephone rang. It was our daughter calling from Kansas City. After saying "Hi" to our little granddaughters and talking to their parents, we were about to hang up when Tami, then four, rushed up to her mother insisting, "I want to say, 'I love you.'" So we talked to our grandchildren once again and heard those magic words which always warm our hearts.

Since then we have acquired another set of granddaughters. Each time we talk to their parents, they, too, have to take their turn via the long distance wire. Darla can say, "I love you" plainly, but Beth Anne's utterance is still in the garbled stage. However, the desire is there and we know it.

If only more people cared enough to say those words, what a different world it would be, I have thought. What a nicer place in which to live!

Love is one commodity that will never overflood the market. It is and always will be in demand, for God is love and He created man in His likeness. Therefore to be loved is an instinctive need. Because of this inherited craving, the girls working in a certain Korean orphanage were required to carry the babies strapped to their backs for two hours daily. The warmth of the nurses' bodies transmitted love and security to the underprivileged infants.

It takes healthy, happy people to make a healthy, happy world. Healthy, happy people need to show their love more.

Jesus Christ, our example, loved. He cared. He spent His earthly sojourn expressing His concern for others. He cared for the heavy-laden; He bid them to come to Him and find rest. He cared for the hungry; He multiplied the loaves and fishes and the people ate until they were filled. He cared for the blind man; He restored his sight. He cared for the bereaved; He restored the dead to life. He cared for the diseased; He healed the suffering. He cared for the adultress; He forgave the woman at the well of her sins.

He cares—still.

Dwight L. Moody said:

> No matter how lowdown you are; no matter what your disposition has been; you may be low in your thoughts, words and actions; you may be selfish; your heart may be overflowing with corruption and wickedness; yet Jesus will have compassion on you. He will speak comforting words to you; not treat you coldly or spurn you, as perhaps those of earth would, but will speak tender words—words of love, affection and kindness. Just come at once. He is a faithful friend—a friend that sticketh closer than a brother.

God loved the world so much He gave up His only begotten Son. His Son, in turn, cared enough to willingly lay down His life for us. We shall be eternally in debt to Him for His sacrifice. The only means we have of reducing this debt is through loving and caring for others in Jesus' name.

Loving and caring for others is an antidote for our own times of depression. When gloom descends on us—and it will—we can find relief through deliberate effort to ease the burden of another. I asked our ever-cheerful funeral director how he keeps from becoming morbid in his work.

Dan replied, "By helping someone else."

N. Dwight Hillis said happiness comes through being helpful to others. He urged building a booth each morning to shelter someone from life's heat, digging some life-spring for thirsty lips each noon, and providing food for the hungry and shelter for the cold and naked each night.

Caring means being on the alert, always watching for an opportunity to smile or cause a heart to beat faster. It means seeking out ways to go beyond the call of duty, to do something that is not expected or required.

We emphasize, and rightly so, the matter of surrender, but holiness is a two-sided coin with surrender on one side and total commitment on the other. Since He has given so freely of himself, it is but the Christian's "reasonable service" to devote his life to serving both young and old in Christ's name. For when we do something for others we are doing it for Him.

We can pray. We can care. We can share. We can let Him move freely through us to help a needy world. We can do as Martyn urged and "burn out" for God.

Missionary Russell Birchard did just that. His body lies bured on foreign soil among the people he loved and cared for, and for whom he labored until his body could stand no more wear.

When the missionary once gave a crippled man a homemade wheelchair, the recipient said, "You're the first man in 18 years who has taken an interest in me."

Other people do not always respond to overtures of love. But my friend Frances had the healthy attitude when she said, "I don't think about whether people like me or not. I love everybody and I figure everyone loves me."

Love is caring. It is being concerned enough to do something about it. Love is given even though it may not be returned. It is shared through our attitudes, deeds, and words.

My six-year-old nephew flopped down on the sofa, grinned, and confided, "Aunt Pauline, you're sure a nice aunt. I like you."

"Well, I love you, too, Billy," I said, stopping my work to give him a bear hug.

"When I get a car, I'm going to come to see you," he promised.

"I love you." Or, "I like you." Great power is in those words. They dispel weariness. They destroy resentments. Many of the world's ills would vanish if we used them more often. Many faults would be overlooked. Many hurts would be forgotten. And goodwill would flow freely. An expression of love fortifies us against the cruelty about us. It brings hope when we feel forlorn and forsaken. It strengthens us to do unpleasant tasks and to keep on going in spite of discouragement.

The mother of a retarded child was worried. How would society accept him as he grew older? But she need not have feared the outcome, for the child learned to greet everyone with the magic words, "I like you."

"Happiness is . . . loving."

Happiness Is . . .

Giving It Away

The following quotation by William A. Ward was taped to Sue's dresser mirror during her teen years. Now, yellow and worn, it reposes between the pages of my Bible.

"Real happiness," said Mr. Ward, "is more of a habit than a goal, more of an attitude than an attainment. It is the companion of cheerfulness, not the creature of circumstance. Happiness is what overtakes us when we forget ourselves, when we learn to open your eyes in optimism and close the coor in the face of defeat. We win happiness when we lose ourselves in service to others."

The early Persian philosopher, Zoroaster, said, "Doing good to others is not a duty. It is a joy, for it increases your own health and happiness."

It has been noted that happiness is a perfume you cannot lavish on others without getting a few drops on yourself.

Jesus said, "Freely ye have received, freely give" (Matt. 10:8).

Years ago we planned to spend Thanksgiving Day with relatives. But at the last minute one of the children became ill and we had to stay home. Disappointed, I began searching for something to do to make my family happy. This would change my own mood, too, I thought. And it did.

Remembering a pattern I had acquired in an art course, I set about to make a "turkey" cake. My creative effort was a huge success as far as we were concerned. Therefore I continued to make turkey-shaped, candy-corn-decorated cakes annually for years afterward. Eventually, I wove a story around the idea and it spread beyond the walls of our parsonage kitchen.

Recently while three-year-old Darla was visiting us, she came into the kitchen smiling. "We're having fun here, aren't we, Mama?" she asked happily. Needless to say, that made us happy, too.

We've heard it said that Christmas is for the children, but love has a way of boomeranging. It blesses and returns to bless. Adults cannot give happiness to youngsters (or oldsters, for that matter) without it coming back to brighten and enrich their own lives.

To be mentally healthy, it has been suggested that we make at least one child happy each day. It takes so little to please children, for they have the wonderful ability to enjoy the simple pleasures of life—a few cookies and a glass of milk, a stick of gum, a card or a letter in the mail.

Excitedly anticipating Christmas, Shari told her Sunday school teacher, "We're going to Grandma's house and I'm going to have cinnamon rolls every morning for breakfast."

A little sunshine brightens a dreary day. A little rain quiets a dusty pathway. A little breeze cools a sweating brow. A little shade refreshes a weary traveler. A little concern encourages the disheartened. A little kindness may save one from despair, or lighten a heavy or discouraged heart.

It doesn't take "big" things to convey the message of love. Nor should our giving of the "little" things be limited to the children. Adults have need of them, too.

The telephone rang. "Ethel died last night," we were told. Quickly our thoughts went back to our pastorate in her church. Never can we forget the happiness this dear soul and her husband brought us. Because of the many "little" kindnesses they bestowed on us, we received "big" blessings. Their acts of thoughtfulness will never be forgotten.

The Zs showed us that "little things" count a lot. One day they brought half a watermelon, sharing it with us, they said, because it was especially sweet. There were cookies—a dozen at a time. Enough blueberries for supper. Generous supplies of vitamin-filled carrot juice, a product of their extractor. And their time and patience.

When my husband was ill, they brought him half a dozen oranges, far nicer ones than we would buy. One Christmas they received a box of California goodies from a son out west. A few days later, some of each of the dates, prunes, and figs found their way to our house. Every now and then there was a knock on our door. It was the Zs with a token of love—squash from their garden, fresh strawberries, pears, cookies, or watermelon. Over and over, our hearts were warmed by their expressions of love and thoughtfulness.

Jesus brought comfort to thousands when He blessed and broke the loaves and fishes. He recognized the potential blessings in a cup of cold water, a lad's lunch, and a comforting word.

Carl Holmes said:

> A happy life is made up of little things in which smiles and small favors are given habitually: a gift sent, a letter written, a call made, a recommendation given, transportation provided, a cake made, a book lent, a check sent—things which are done without hesitation. Kindness isn't sacrifice so much as it is being considerate for the feelings of others, sharing happiness, the unsel-

fish thought, the spontaneous and friendly act, forgetfulness of our own present interests.

Time or space does not permit the listing of all the little things we can find to do for others. Writing a letter is a little thing, but Solomon said, "As cold waters to a thirsty soul, so is good news from a far country" (Prov. 25:25). A compliment or word of praise is a little thing, but "a word fitly spoken is like apples of gold in pictures of silver" (Prov. 25:11).

Sincere praise inspires others to greater accomplishments. Humanity reaches its highest degree of excellence when it is the recipient of human and divine appreciation. Often a word of praise or encouragement produces a greater healing effect than the most potent medicines.

The ability to give praise is not a sign of weakness, but of strength.

"You've been a good mother to us," her children said as they were gathered around the bedside of the dying woman.

"You never told me that before," she whispered with her final breath.

Don't let people die from a lack of recognition, commendation, or a bit of praise. Help others live. In doing so, you, too, will experience joy.

"There is no happiness in having and getting," said F. W. Gunsaulus, "but only in giving. Half the world is on the wrong scent in pursuit of happiness."

Ray Lyman Wilbur noted, "Unless we think of others and do something for them, we miss one of the greatest sources of happiness."

"Happiness is . . . giving it away."

Happiness Is . . .

Making the Best of It

Karl Humboldt said, "I am more and more convinced that our happiness or unhappiness depends far more on the way we meet the events of life, than on the nature of those events themselves."

Queen Mother Elizabeth of England and her husband preferred to live a quiet life. However, when the duties of the throne were thrust upon them, she declared simply, "We will have to make the best of it!"

Again, when their first-born, Elizabeth, married and left them, she said, "We will have to make the best of it!"

None of us, regardless of our station, can control all the circumstances that come in life. We only have the privilege of deciding what attitude we shall take toward what comes.

The trusting Christian believes that "all things work together for good to them that love God" (Rom. 8:28). Having confidence that this is true makes practicing the queen mother's philosophy much easier.

No life is ideal, but as Abraham Lincoln said, "Most folks are about as happy as they make up their minds to be."

Every life is filled with frustrations and challenges.

Every Christian has a cross to bear. No one gets to heaven without a struggle. We can whine, cringe, and shrivel up spiritually. Or, we can turn our minuses into pluses by taking an optimistic attitude toward them.

I resisted wholeheartedly the idea of moving into a rented home while the church people sought a buyer for the parsonage. My resistance put me in a state of stress. When I decided to accept the idea and go along as if it were some new adventure, my tensions ceased. (And, incidentally, the proposal was dropped.)

One lady's husband insisted on decorating the walls of their home according to his tastes. When I voiced my sympathy and insisted she was being denied her womanly right, she answered sweetly, "Well, if I don't get the paper I want, I just begin to think of ways to fix up the house so it will look nice." She has learned the secret of living peaceably. Contentedly. Happily.

We need to apply the queen mother's philosophy when it comes to people, also. We run into countless troubles when we try to change others to our liking. If perchance we are successful, we are prone to discover later that we liked them better the way they were originally.

After 30-some years of living with my husband, I have come to accept him as he is. My nagging has declined with the years, I hope. I no longer complain about the way he drips the egg white on the cook range. (Most women would give a lot to have their husbands cook their own breakfasts.) When he says "helt" instead of "held," I realize it only adds to his uniqueness and charm. After all, he acquired his O.B. (Oklahoma brogue) long before I received my MRS.

Although it may be difficult, we need to learn to "make the best" of those things which do not measure up to the ideals we have formed in our minds. Everything does not have to be exactly as we pictured it to be. Everything does not have to be "just perfect."

Some persons, especially those who are strongly melancholic, create mental images of what people and circumstances *should* be like. These impressions come from reading, from the suggestions of others, and from observation. When reality differs from their ideals, these persons are disappointed.

We must remember that God sometimes chooses to use unconventional means through which to work. Therefore, we had better learn to "make the best" of what comes lest we thwart His plan.

Then, too, we need to "make the best" of our own infirmities. If one failed to inherit a robust constitution, there is no need to let it hinder him from living usefully.

Countless individuals have inherited temperamental qualities which make them "allergic" to above-normal tension. They simply cannot "take" as much pressure as their brother or sister can. They give out quicker when it comes to expending mental and emotional energy. Still, this does not mean they cannot enjoy a profitable existence.

Eileen Farrell, the operatic singer, said, "You have to know your limitations and operate within them. . . . Some roles I wouldn't attempt—such as Madame Butterfly. It is not for my voice, and I don't look the part. I would be ridiculous."

This applies exactly to the person who has limited nervous strength. He needs to understand himself well enough to know how much he can or cannot take. Looks can be most deceiving. Just because one is "the picture of health" does not necessarily make it so.

It is a gross error to believe that the size of an individual determines his degree of nervous strength. Some pint-sized persons can outlast others twice their size. Furthermore, many who are housed in large bodies possess sensitive emotional makeups. When they break down, they are vastly misunderstood and often unjustly criticized.

Through experimentation and experience, each must ascertain how much he can take without overtaxing his strength. Then he must adjust his life accordingly. It may mean to work awhile and rest awhile. How long to work and how long to rest will have to be determined by the individual.

If one is born with the ability to "put out" less, one should strive to make quality count. If one's nerves give out occasionally, one must find consolation in knowing that it is quality, not quantity, that matters most.

Furthermore, we can learn to make substitutions. If we can't run, we must learn to walk. If we can't plow, the Lord may want us to punch typewriter keys. Or vice versa. We will not give up when one avenue is closed. We will simply take another route.

A host of people have triumphed over seemingly insurmountable odds. Uncle Bud Robinson was a sought-after speaker despite a speech impediment. Helen Keller made a profound contribution to mankind in spite of combined blindness and deafness. Hymnwriters, poets, artists, civic leaders, and preachers have made the world richer despite infirmities.

"There was a man named Zacchaeus" also. He was a rich man, in high standing and influential. But he had a problem. What did he do?

Zacchaeus made his limitation, his shortness of stature, count. He ran ahead and climbed up in a tree. Had it not been for his "minus point," he would not have met the Master face-to-face as he did.

Let us never forget that "the Spirit . . . helpeth our infirmities" (Rom. 8:26), and the Lord uses the weak things of this world to confound the mighty (1 Cor. 1:27).

"Happiness is . . . making the best of it."

Happiness Is . . .

Hanging On

Happiness in this world, when it comes, comes incidentally. Make it the object of pursuit, and it leads us on a wild-goose chase, and is never attained," said Nathaniel Hawthorne.

Happiness is a by-product. For one thing, it comes as the result of working with the right motives. The Christian's highest purpose should be to glorify God. Paul said, "Whether therefore ye eat, or drink, or whatsoever ye do, do all to the glory of God" (1 Cor. 10:31).

Glorifying God is a lifelong adventure which calls for the continual exercising of faith, for "by faith ye stand" (2 Cor. 1:24).

Not all of life is smooth sailing. Sometimes we may wonder if we shall ever be happy again. But steadfast confidence in God has its reward.

"You wanna help me set out strawberry plants in the morning?" my dad asked when I was home visiting.

The next morning I donned borrowed gardening clothes and we set out to a neighbor's house to dig up some runners and reset them in a plot behind the tool shed.

There Dad had driven two sticks into the ground, one

at either end of the row. To these sticks he fastened his marking line. Because he lacked a length of binder twine long enough to stretch the length of the row, he tied many pieces of used twine together.

Glancing down the row, I was reminded of the quotation: "When you get to the end of your rope, tie a knot and hang on."

Since then I've recalled many times in my life when I have done just that—tied a knot of faith and hung on.

During my youth, when I discovered to my disillusionment and dismay that a teen-aged friend was not the Christian I had believed her to be, I tied a knot and hung on.

When, in the "lean" years of our early married life, we sought help from Christian friends whom we trusted implicitly, and were declined assistance, we tied a knot and hung on.

When one we admired as a child of God not only let God down but brought embarrassment to His kingdom, we tied a knot and hung on.

When a young father was tragically killed in a farm accident, it was natural to wonder "Why?" But we tied a knot and hung on.

When other friends died in the prime of life, leaving their children motherless and we were asked "Why?" we tied a knot of faith and hung on.

When we moved to a new church, thinking we were getting a promotion only to discover to our chagrin a situation which proved to be most discouraging (albeit challenging), we tied a knot and hung on.

When a confidence was broken by one we trusted, we tied a knot and hung on.

When physical strength failed and when nerves became exhausted, we tied a knot and hung on.

When rejection slips were more numerous than publishers' checks, we tied a knot and hung on.

When going through spiritual dry spells when it seemed God did not hear and no feeling was present, we tied a knot and hung on.

"Cast not away . . . your confidence," cautioned the writer to the Hebrews (10:35).

Faith changes people. Faith changes circumstances. Faith changes our outlook. Faith alters our emotions. Faith brings the victory. Faith *is* the victory. Steadfast confidence is rewarded!

The next time you are convinced that you will never be happy again, remember: "Weeping may endure for a night, but joy cometh in the morning" (Ps. 30:5).

"Happiness is . . . hanging on."

Reference Notes

1. Andrew Blackwood, *Preaching from the Bible* (Nashville: Abingdon-Cokesbury Press, 1941), p. 160.

2. Hannah Whitall Smith, *The Christian's Secret of a Happy Life* (Westwood, N.J.: Fleming H. Revell Co., reprint, 1952), p. 7.

3. "Your Spiritual Workshop," *Guideposts* (Carmel, N.Y.: Guideposts Associates, Inc.), Sept., 1964.

4. Brother Lawrence, *His Conversations and Letters on the Practice of the Presence of God* (Cincinnati: Forward Movement Publications, n.d.), Foreword.

5. L. Guy Nees, "The Personal Dimension," *Herald of Holiness* (Kansas City: Nazarene Publishing House), Feb. 12, 1969.

6. Cecil G. Osborne, *The Art of Understanding Yourself* (Grand Rapids: Zondervan Publishing House, 1967).

7. S. D. Gordon, *Quiet Talks on Personal Problems* (New York: Fleming H. Revell Co., 1910), p. 101.

8. *Ibid.*, p. 114.

9. Mary McSherry, "Why Some Men Live Longer," *Woman's Day* (New York: Fawcett Publications), Oct., 1971, p. 6.

10. S. D. Gordon, *Quiet Talks on Service* (New York: Fleming H. Revell Co., 1906), p. 167.

11. Gordon, *Quiet Talks on Personal Problems*, p. 113.

12. J. B. McClure, *Pearls from Many Seas* (Chicago: Rhodes and McClure Publishing Co., 1909), pp. 332-33.

13. William S. Sadler, *Theory and Practice of Psychiatry* (St. Louis: The C. V. Mosby Co., 1936), p. 681.

Bibliography and Resources

Bartlett, John. *The Shorter Bartlett's Familiar Quotations*. New York: Permabooks, 1953.

Blackwood, Andrew. *Preaching from the Bible*. Nashville: Abingdon-Cokesbury Press, 1941.

Brother Lawrence. *His Conversations and Letters on the Practice of the Presence of God*. Cincinnati: Forward Movement Publications, n.d.

Brown, Will H. *Illustrative Incidents for Public Speakers*. Cincinnati: The Standard Publishing Co., 1915.

Browns, Ralph Emerson. *The New Dictionary of Thoughts*. Standard Book Company, 1959.

Burgess, Perry. *Who Walk Alone*. New York: Holt, Rinehart, and Winston, Inc., 1940.

Deal, William S. *Problems of the Spirit-filled Life*. Kansas City: Beacon Hill Press, 1961.

Douglas, Mack R. *How to Make a Habit of Succeeding*. Grand Rapids: Zondervan Publishing House, 1966.

Gordon, S. D. *Quiet Talks on Personal Problems*. New York: Fleming H. Revell Co., 1910.

———. *Quiet Talks on Service*. New York: Fleming H. Revell Co., 1906.

Guideposts. Carmel, N.Y. Sept., 1964, and Dec., 1951.

Henry, Lewis C. *Best Quotations for All Occasions*. Greenwich, Conn.: Fawcett Publications, Inc., 1955.

Lytle, Clyde Francis. *Leaves of Gold*. Williamsport, Pa.: The Coslett Publishing Co., 1948.

Maltz, Maxwell. *Psycho-Cybernetics*. New York: Prentice-Hall, Inc., 1960.

McClure, J. B. *Pearls from Many Seas*. Chicago: Rhodes and McClure Publishing Co., 1909.

McSherry, Mary. "Why Some Men Live Longer." *Woman's Day.* New York: Fawcett Publications, Oct., 1971.

Nees, L. Guy. "The Personal Dimension." *Herald of Holiness.* Kansas City: Nazarene Publishing House, Feb. 12, 1969.

Osborne, Cecil G. *The Art of Understanding Yourself.* Grand Rapids: Zondervan Publishing House, 1967.

Sadler, William S. *Theory and Practice of Psychiatry.* St. Louis: The C. V. Mosby Co., 1936.

Sangster, W. E. "Forget It!—And How." *Reader's Digest.* Pleasantville, New York: The Reader's Digest Association, Inc., Dec., 1951. (Reprinted from *Guideposts.* New York: Guideposts Associates, Inc., Dec., 1951).

Smith, Hannah Whitall. *The Christian's Secret of a Happy Life.* Westwood, N.J.: Fleming H. Revell Co., 1952.

Taylor, Richard S. *The Disciplined Life.* Kansas City: Beacon Hill Press, 1962.

Treasury of Familiar Quotations (Avenel Books). New York: Crown Publishers, Inc., 1955.

Watson, Lillian Eichler. *Light from Many Lamps.* New York: Simon and Schuster, 1951.

Zepp, Arthur C. *Progress After Entire Sanctification.* Chicago: The Christian Witness Co., 1909.